SUPER JACK

SUPER JACK

The Jack Grealish Story - Britain's First £100m Player

By

SIMON GOODYEAR

Published in 2021 by G2 Entertainment
www.g2books.co.uk

Copyright © 2021 G2 Entertainment

ISBN (Paperback): 978-1-78281-478-8
ISBN (eBook): 978-1-78281-479-5

Written by Simon Goodyear

Front cover design Paul Briggs

Book design Alex Young

Publishers Jules Gammond & Edward Adams

Printed and bound in the UK

ABOUT THE AUTHOR

It all started by chance really, shortly after my father, a life-long Aston Villa and England fan, passed away in the autumn of 2008. While searching through my father's house, I discovered a scruffy, old plastic bag with what appeared to be a t-shirt in it. On closer inspection, I discovered it was an old England football shirt with a number '9' on the back. Not knowing who this 1960s' football shirt belonged to, I later discovered a host of old photos and identified the person as the late Gerry Hitchens. Putting two and two together, I assumed the England shirt also belonged to the ex-Aston Villa, Inter Milan, and England legend who died in 1983. Indeed, it did. What was my father doing with these historical items? Little did I know back then just what treasure I'd discovered and how it would change my life – but it was all good.

It didn't take long for me to contact the Hitchens family, and a few weeks later I returned the photos and the England shirt to their rightful home. However, it wasn't by coincidence that the shirt was in my father's possession; my father was in fact a friend of the Hitchens family, and was in the process of trying to get the shirt displayed in a museum.

In the meantime, I had gained the permission of the family to write Gerry's long-awaited biography. Not having any experience in writing, I set about the task of trying to fill a book with the memories of his family and information taken from newspaper articles, which had been compiled by my father. It could be said that I went into it 'blind', but no more than six months later, and after many trips to North Wales to interview Gerry's widow, Meriel, and eldest son, Marcus, a book was published called, *'The Gerry Hitchens Story: From Mine to Milan'*. The rest, as they say, is history.

Much publicity was secured from the publication of the book (and the subsequent discovery of rare 8mm cine film shot by Gerry Hitchens during the 1962 World Cup in Chile), including appearances on the BBC, Sky Sports, and talkSPORT radio, as well as a host of local and national radio shows and newspapers, it did not take long for me to acquire a taste and passion for writing. Incidentally that England shirt is now being displayed in the **FA Football Museum in Manchester**.

In the years that followed I've written more books, and my latest documents the life stories of football legends Peter Withe (2017) and Brian Little (2018).

This book about Jack Grealish was a pleasure to write, a player I have admired as a fan for seven or eight years, a player who in my opinion has become the best English footballer since Paul Gascoigne, and that's the biggest compliment I can give, because 'Gazza' was just a fabulous footballer.

He is now Britain's most expensive footballer.

Simon Goodyear
www.goodyearpublications.com

ALSO, BY THE AUTHOR

Gerry Hitchens: From Mine to Milan
Bobby Thomson: The Real Bobby Dazzler
La Storia di Gerry Hitchens (Italian edition)
The Harry Moseley Story – Making It Happen
Memories Made in Aston
Peter Withe: All for the Love of the Game
Cherno Samba: Still in the Game
Brian Little: A Little is Enough
An A-Z of Aston Villa

ACKNOWLEDGMENTS & REFERENCES

I would like to thank Jules Gammond and G2 Books for the opportunity to write this biography of Jack Grealish. It was a great pleasure to write about one of England's most talented and exciting footballers around at the moment, a player who must be the future of the England national side for years to come.

I would like to thank another good friend, David Shuttle, who kindly offered to edit the manuscript before it was ready to be sent to the publishers. Thank you David.

A thank you also goes to fellow Villa fan, radio presenter and good friend of mine, Jonny Gould for his time and effort in sense-checking the manuscript before it went to be edited. Thank you Jonny.

Finally, another big thank you to Ellie Shepherd, who proof-read the manuscript before it was submitted to G2 Books.

During the writing of this book, the following references were used from the internet:

Birmingham Live	The Telegraph
Goal.com	beIN Sports
Tribal Football	Sky Sports News
BBC Football	Express & Star
Givemesport	AVTV
AVFC.co.uk	Oxford Mail
Nottingham Post	London Evening Standard
Premierleague.com	The Independent
The Metro	Soccerbible
talentaintenough.co.uk	Mirror.co.uk
Manchester Evening News	

CONTENTS

PROLOGUE

Former Aston Villa captain, Jack Grealish has the world at his feet at the time of writing, but it hasn't been all plain sailing for the 26-year-old, super-talented midfielder.

He has come a long way since his loan spell with Notts County in 2013 as a skinny 18-year-old. After making his full Villa debut in the 2014 - 2015 season, Jack came to life in the FA Cup semi-final against Liverpool and helped his side progress to the final. However, Villa lost that final and were relegated from the Premier League in the following season.

Playing under the radar in the Championship for three seasons, Jack found his talents were mainly hidden from the wider world; however, the Villa faithful all knew he was a diamond in the making. It's no coincidence that Jack's favourite player when he was very young was Paul Merson, a former Villa playmaker himself and a footballer who oozed class and you can see that the way Jack plays certainly has shades of 'Merse'.

Coming back from a long-term injury and becoming Villa captain in March 2019 seemed to be the making of him as Jack led Villa to a record 10 straight wins and led the club back into the big-time by helping his side win the EFL Championship Play-Off Final at Wembley.

Suddenly, 'Super Jack' has attracted the attention of football fans right across the country (and the world) and he became the most talked about footballer in Europe; he became the most sought-after player on the planet, with all the top clubs looking at his next move.

Jack Grealish belongs in the Premier League and it was no fluke that he led his Villa side to victory in May 2019, and subsequently managed to cling on to their Premier League status on the final day of their first season.

England beckoned and eventually he got his chance, making his full international debut in September 2020, and being picked for Euro 2020 (which was played in the summer of 2021). It would take a brave man to take that number 7 shirt away from him.

Watch this space - there's more to come from Jack Grealish, that's for certain.

Chapter 1

COMETH THE HOUR, COMETH THE MAN

How Jack Grealish steered Villa to a famous play-off victory.

Bank Holiday Monday, 27th May 2019 will go down in history as the day Aston Villa returned to the big-time of the Premier League. It will be a day all Villa fans will remember forever, not least because the club was being managed by Dean Smith and skippered by Jack Grealish, both die-hard, Birmingham born Villa fans.

If you don't believe in miracles or dreams coming true, then both of those events happened for Villa fans that day, at the 'Theatre of Dreams' – Wembley Stadium on that warm and sunny day in May.

For Jack Grealish, it will be the day that he announced himself to the world - and made a statement to the doubters that he certainly is, the real deal.

They say that the EFL Championship Play-Off Final is the richest club football game in the world, and rightly so, because the prize is a place in the Premier League, arguably the biggest stage in world club football. Of all those clubs who desperately wanted to get into the Premier League at the end of the 2018 – 2019 season, Aston Villa were probably the club that deserved to be there the most. Maybe it's the long, rich history as being one of England's most successful clubs - or maybe it's my sheer biased opinion?

One thing was certain, promotion would end a three-year exile and return Villa to what they believed was their rightful place. As the club's moto suggests, Villa were 'Prepared' in 2019, unlike a year before, when it was desperation more than hope. And for Jack Grealish, it was the only place he wanted to be, and a place he belonged - and some may say it was written in the stars.

You see, miracles do happen – and I believe in them, because I was there to witness it!

****

After the turbulent 12 months in the history of Aston Villa Football Club, getting to the EFL Championship Play-Off Final was a miracle of incredible proportions. Aston Villa was a club that had nearly gone bust literally 12 months before the biggest game in the club's history, certainly since the European Cup Final in 1982. And I mean literally on the brink of administration; the money had run out for their (then) owner, Dr Tony Xia and the club were struggling both on and off the pitch. It seemed that manager Steve Bruce had been used as a scapegoat for all things that went wrong on the pitch, but by 27th May 2019, he and Dr Xia had gone, and the excuses had run out.

Football fans are a fickle bunch at the best (and worst of times), but to be fair to Villa fans they had a torrid time for the best part of 10 years, ever since Martin O'Neill walked out on the cusp of the 2010 - 2011 season, leaving a gaping hole in the club. The appointment of Dean Smith in October 2018 seemed to galvanise the Villa faithful at last and the vast majority were happy to see 'one of our own' be appointed as manager of our football club.

However, Villa were stuck in mid-table during most of 2018, and a shin injury to Jack Grealish in the December almost shattered the hopes and dreams of the Villa fans for another season. The very mention of being in the final as late into the season as March 2019 would have been viewed as pie-in-the sky, with the Villa faithful holding only a glimmer of hope of reaching the play-offs, let alone the final itself.

Fast forward just a few months, Villa seemed like a totally different club; a progressive club, and a club that had gone through a root and branch change from top to bottom, both on and off the pitch. The new multi-billionaire owners had pumped millions into the club and spent big money during the summer and winter transfer windows.

Jack's return from injury couldn't have come quick enough, but even the Villa faithful wouldn't have dreamed of what happened in the final dozen or so games of the season. However, the biggest event that changed the season was the surprising decision Dean Smith made prior to Jack's long-awaited return from four months on the side-lines, a reaction that shocked even the most die-hardest Villa fan.

'Super Jack' was made captain. Yes, out of the blue, Jack had been catapulted into leading his troops out for the final leg of the Championship season and nobody had seen that coming – not least Jack himself.

The reaction from the media and the Villa fans was a mixture confusion and sheer delight; Dean Smith was either mad or knew exactly what he was doing.

However, in hindsight it was a masterstroke, but at the time it was seen as a major gamble, but whatever it was, it paid off. By the time Jack led his Villa team out for the eleventh time at Elland Road on 28th April, Villa had secured a record 10 back-to-back victories and a play-off semi-final double-header against local rivals, West Bromwich Albion that seemed unlikely at best only two months previously.

Of course, Villa beat West Bromwich Albion, but only after a nail-biting second-leg tie that went all the way to penalties.

That was part one of the miracle. Part two was just around the corner.

As in all games, there are two clubs involved and Derby County had a similar agenda and were waiting in the wings to shatter Villa's dreams. Derby had beaten Leeds, the favourites for automatic promotion at the start of the season, over two legs and their manager, Frank Lampard wasn't bothered with the journey Villa had in getting so close to achieving their dreams. For the Villa fans though, the expectation of winning was so much higher than it was 12 months previously when Villa were beaten by Fulham. They were nervously dreaming of the Premier League and not even contemplating losing.

There was unfinished business after the bad memories of the previous season. Even before the final, the owners had planned for two scenarios: one with Jack and one without him. In other words, win and keep Jack, lose and he would be more than likely have to be sold; it was all about money and getting to the Premier League was the be all and end all for the owners. Losing wasn't an option, well it was, but the consequences weren't worth thinking about. Everyone at the club knew the importance of that one game, but it wasn't quite as bad as win or bust, as it was 12 months previously. According to Dean Smith speaking to the media before the big day, "One way or another, on Monday night we will either be a Premier League team, or a Championship team and you have to have two scenarios for it. But the difference this year is that the owners we've got are fully behind the club and it's on an even keel and hopefully moving in an upwards direction."

However, much of the talk before the big day surrounded Jack Grealish and the prospects of him staying at Villa if the unthinkable happened for the second year in a row – that they lose a play-off final again. Dean Smith insisted that he wouldn't let his prized asset leave "on the cheap" if Villa lost to Derby County at Wembley. Having fought off Tottenham Hotspur only 12 months previously, they were seen as the most likely club to express another interest in Jack, should Villa lose. Smith made it clear to any potential buyer that to capture Jack would come at a very substantial price, "If we don't go up, he'll cost someone a hell of a lot of money if they want to buy him. He's committed to Aston Villa and we've not even spoken about it otherwise." Smith told The Guardian.

On the flipside, if Villa won the tie, it would be a whole lot easier to keep Jack.

The other talking point before the big game was around Villa being a 'one-man team' and all the pressure being on Jack to perform and steer his side into the Premier League. Of course, that was the media saying that, but Dean Smith made it clear that he had other star names in his side, the likes of John McGinn, Anwar El Ghazi, Tyrone Mings and their goal-machine, Tammy Abraham, "We won't put any pressure on any individual and talking of Jack, he doesn't feel that either, He has relished being captain of Aston Villa and is looking forward to the game and hopefully getting that win."

Jack Grealish and his Aston Villa team-mates were 90 minutes away from the 'promised land' of the Premier League, a return to the place a club the size and stature of Villa were meant to be. There was no doubt that Jack wanted nothing more than to see his team back in the big time. Dean Smith was under no illusion how important Jack was in the Villa team and saw him as the ideal player to lead the team out at Wembley, "It will be unbelievable for him and he wants nothing more than to get promoted with Aston Villa," Dean Smith told the Telegraph before the final. "He has relished being the captain and is looking forward to the game and hopefully getting that win. It will mean everything to him. There could be pressure on him but that is something right from the off we have played down. We won't put any pressure on any individual and talking to Jack he doesn't feel that either."

Before the game, the advantage was with Villa, who had already scored seven goals during the season, so that record held them in good stead going into the final. However, Villa had lost their previous four finals at Wembley.

It was all set for a cracker of a game; a Midlands derby and a game no team could really afford to lose. That's why the club had prepared for both scenarios.

By the age of 23, Jack had already made three appearances for Villa at Wembley and the 27th May 2019 was his fourth, but first as captain. Amongst those thousands of fans were more than 30 of Jack's family members – including five who had flown in from Australia. Thoughts of his grandmother, Maggie, who had passed away in April 2019, were not far from his mind.

As for his manager, Dean Smith, he had his own personal pressures, his father, also a lifelong Villa fan, was suffering from dementia and was unaware that his son was managing their club.

Not only did Jack face the pressure of playing in front of his own family but he had the added pressure of playing in front of a member of THE most famous family in the world, and a Villa fan as well. The

Duke of Cambridge, Prince William himself, was at Wembley to watch his team so the pressure really was on 'Super Jack' to perform, by Royal command.

Cometh the hour, cometh the man!

Ahead of the game, Dean Smith named a familiar starting line-up, with the likes of Tyrone Mings, John McGinn, Jack Grealish and Tammy Abraham all included. Meanwhile, Derby manager, Frank Lampard, made two changes to the side that beat Leeds United 4 - 2 at Elland Road in the semi-final, second leg, with Ashley Cole starting in place of the suspended Scott Malone, and Tom Huddlestone recalled in midfield.

Jack was in the game from the start as Villa came out of the traps the quickest, with Conor Hourihane controlling a miskick from Derby keeper Kelle Roos and setting Grealish away, only for the midfielder to fire over. Minutes later, McGinn tried one of his trademark volleys from the edge of the area but dragged his shot wide.

There were few chances in the first half and Derby were struggling to break down the Villa defence. Then, in the 33rd minute, Tammy Abraham picked up the ball and ran at the Rams' back-line, shooting narrowly over. However, their next chance did bring a goal when an inviting cross from the right by Ahmed Elmohamady was met by Anwar El Ghazi, who got in front of his man and stooped to head Villa into the lead. Just before the break it was 1 – 0 to Villa.

There were also few chances at the start of the second half, although both sides were giving their all, at least until the 59th minute. That man, Anwar El Ghazi was involved again, as his cross looped into the air and looked like a simple catch for Roos, but McGinn gambled and just beat the keeper to the ball to head Villa into a two-goal lead. Villa were in heaven and seemed like they were cruising to victory. They didn't hold off either after scoring their second and came forward again, with Jack firing wide from the edge of the area.

Lampard rolled the dice with just over 20 minutes remaining, there was a moment of promise for Derby, as Jayden Bogle surged forward and hit the side-netting. The Rams were turning up the heat on the Villa defence, with a corner causing chaos inside the area, and eventually the pressure paid off. A cross was knocked down into the path of Jack Marriott, who made no mistake in finding the corner and setting up a nervous finale. If the Duke of Cambridge was biting his nails, then every Villa fan inside Wembley and sitting at home watching was too. Prince William was seen on TV with his head in his hands towards the end of the 90 minutes, not able to watch, but despite Derby's best efforts in the closing stages it was Villa's day.

Aston Villa 2 Derby County 1

In the end, it was the Villa fans who were making all the noise, singing along with 'Sweet Caroline' and 'Hi Ho Silver Lining' which could be heard serenading out of the PA system and Villa fans celebrated for over an hour after the final whistle.

"It feels right that Aston Villa are in the Premier League," Smith told the Telegraph.

The Villans were going up, and the party had only just getting started.

The game couldn't have gone any better and life couldn't have been any sweeter for Jack, and he summed it up beautifully, "That was the best day of my life", he told AVTV. "It's hard to describe my emotions really. But it's just honestly the best day of my life. I went up to see my family after the game and it was all a bit emotional. At the start of the season, I didn't even think I was going to be here. Then I've played at the start of the season, got injured for a while, come back and been given the armband. Then we've gone on an unbeaten winning streak and then here we are now with this little baby – the EFL Championship Play-Off Final trophy. Captaining this club back to where it belongs is honestly a dream come true."

It was also the day Jack Grealish finally arrived on the world football scene, and in spectacular fashion. It really was the stuff that dreams were made of and the making of fantastic memories.

It was also just the start of the Jack Grealish Story!

Chapter 2

A STAR IS BORN

You can see in the way Jack plays, there is a bit of Paul Merson that inspired his style.

Many a young kid wants to be a footballer when they grow up and for a young Jack Grealish, playing football was always about enjoyment every time the ball was at his feet. When Jack was growing up, he used to look up at the Villa stars like Juan Pablo Angel, Benito Carbone and Gabby Agbonlahor – they were all idols to Jack.

Jack was always going to be a Villa fan, and of course, Gabby Agbonlahor, another self-proclaimed Villa fan, was the man of the moment back at the end of the 20th century. Just as Jack is twenty years later. However, Jack's biggest idol was another Villa favourite, and probably one of the most exciting players to grace Villa Park this century 'Magic Man' Paul Merson. He soon became a role model for the four-year-old Jack. It was no surprise to his family, that Jack was going to follow in his footsteps one day.

Jack's introduction to Villa Park was to watch a pulsating FA Cup tie against Leeds United, which was screened live on national TV. Villa won that game, 3 – 2, and that Villa side included the likes of Paul Merson and Benito Carbone, who incidentally scored a wonderful hat-trick that day. Villa's captain was the present England manager, Gareth Southgate.

According to Jack's father, Kevin, they always had a season ticket for Villa and sat in the Witton Land Stand (AKA, The Doug Ellis

Stand), "He always been passionate about it. It's something he has always loved (watching the Villa)", he told Birmingham Live. "I can remember his joining in with all of the chants but he had to be careful because we didn't want him to join in the swearing. We used to change it around a bit to get rid of all the naughty words."

In an interview for AVTV, Jack told one of his Villa idols, Juan Pablo Angel, "I had a season ticket since I was four and used to watch all the games. I used to love getting to the ground early and watching you guys warm up and train. I'd be at the front with my cousins, dreaming about being on the pitch."

Just over year later, in 2001, casual observers in the Solihull area of the West Midlands were admiring the silky skills of an unknown six-year-old kid called Jack Grealish, who, even at that tender age, seemed to run with the ball glued to his feet.

One summer's evening, Jack's father, Kevin, a life-long Villa fan, spotted a man wearing a 'Highgate United Youth' shirt at the nearby Hall Green Greyhound Stadium (now demolished) and immediately started chatting to him about his six-year-old son. That man was the Highgate's coach, Richard Sweeney and he sold the club to Kevin and invited his son to a trial at Kings' Heath Park in South Birmingham. In fact, Richard also invited another four lads of the same age to the trial, including Jack's older cousin.

Speaking to The Mirror, Sweeney explained that they had reservations about Jack at first. However, those reservations evaporated when Jack, whose shinpads covered his knees, started displaying his skills by performing keepie-uppies in front of him. He said: "It all began when Jack's dad asked if his son could train with his cousin, who was with us. His cousin was a year older so I thought Jack was going to struggle. But he rocked up in his Villa kit and his shin pads which were too big for him and up by his knees. Then he suddenly started juggling the ball right in front of us. We thought, 'OK, he is a bit good'. He played with the age group above but was not out of place at all. When he did play in his age group, everything was too easy for him."

All five lads were signed up that day, including Jack.

Sweeney explained, "As a kid he was far better than anything we had seen before. I remember his last game for us, the match was level and the keeper has rolled the ball out to him, he has dribbled around the whole of their team and smashed it in the back of the net. My main recollection is I was worried the first three or four games because he was so young. However, once he sorted out what he had to do, he went from struggling a bit to being the best player. He worked out for himself what he had to do to play at the higher level. He understands football."

Highgate were an old, run-down football club (founded in 1948) and in desperate need of financial help and at that time, the team didn't have a shirt sponsor, but a local family car sales firm called Smallbone Car Sales, run by Villa fan, Martin Smallbone soon changed that. Aided by Martin's schoolteacher wife Lucy and one of Jack's friend's parents, a deal was struck for Smallbone Car Sales to sponsor the team and buy the shirts for £200. Martin was a decent footballer himself so it was a no-brainer for him to sponsor them.

Even as a smiling six-year-old, Jack had a wonderful desire to play football for fun. Jack played one season at Highgate and that was it, not that he got fed up, but because he was spotted by Aston Villa's former scout, Jim Thomas. According to Jim, he was asked to go to watch the Highgate United on a cold and wet Sunday morning in 2002 and to "keep an eye out" for a certain six-year-old lad playing in a six-a-side game. Jim was impressed with young Jack, who turned on the style that day at Tythe Barn Lane in Shirley, Solihull, "You couldn't fail to miss him", Jim told the Birmingham Mail. "As soon as I got there he's got the ball in his own penalty area and dribbled right the way through the team. He was very small. It was like looking at Maradona! There was a lady walking around with a push chair, a pram, and it was his mother Karen and I said, 'I've come to have a look at your son, would he like to come to Villa?' She puffed out her cheeks and said, 'I'll say he would!'. He's go to practise twice a week at Bodymoor and he's never looked back. His family are marvellous people, they took him all the time." Jim quickly snapped up Jack and signed him up for the Villa Academy as someone to keep an eye on.

Apparently, Birmingham City were also looking at Jack, as were a whole host of teams including West Bromwich Albion, but there was no way he was going to go to anywhere other than Aston Villa. There was a picture of Jack taken in 2002, he is seen wearing the shirt, clearly two sizes too big for him. No one back then could have imagined what lay in store for Jack, even 10 years on from that.

Jim was something of a Grade A talent spotter for Villa, he also spotted the likes of Mark Walters, Dean Sturridge and Lee Sharpe 'back in the day'. More recently, Andre Green, Easah Suliman, Jack Clarke and Callum O'Hare.

That was just the start of Jack's journey to the top.

****

Jack Grealish was several years ahead of his peers at school, Our Lady of Compassion Catholic Primary School in Solihull, making the school football team as an eight-year-old. At a school that encouraged all sports, Jack was good at most of them, but it was football where he stood out.

Even at that tender age, he apparently had wonderful balance and superb close control, even though he was slight in stature and small in size. Those two features of his game stood out even back then, but they are also the key features of his game now he's a 'superstar'. You can see from watching him in a Villa or England shirt, he doesn't lose the ball easily and that tells you he hasn't lost any of his raw talent he showed as an eight or nine-year-old kid, kicking the ball around the school playing field.

The kids at his school were always encouraged to be positive, keep trying and keep working hard if they wanted to improve, and while some fell by the wayside, Jack led by example and pushed himself harder than anyone else and continued to improve - there's no real surprise that Jack was made captain of Aston Villa in 2019. I guess Jack was just like any other football-loving kid in the country, that he just loved playing. He also understood that football is a team game and doesn't belong to one individual on the pitch. You don't normally associate young kids with being team-players; most want to outshine their mates and want to score goals themselves. Jack was different in that respect. According to his games' teacher in an interview with Birmingham Live. Jack had a great attitude and always wanted to win. You can see that in him now, and the unselfishness in his game and he always looks for a pass rather than try and score himself.

According to Jack's former primary school head teacher, Chris Bentley, it was a case of "what you see is what you get with Jack. There's no side to him and he's a very honest and hard-working lad. He realises he can make a difference, not just on the pitch, but by his attitude, by his work-rate and by being positive."

It was evident from an early age at Aston Villa's academy that Jack Grealish was no robotic footballer that was churned out of a Premier League production line. Jack had a certain way about him from a young age, and this was clearly demonstrated by his 'trademark' rolled down socks which started early in his football career.

As with most young, talented sportspeople, Jack's parents had an influence on his life. Speaking to AVTV, Jack said, "For my whole life, my parents pushed me; all I ever wanted to do was to be a professional footballer. It was always Villa that I wanted to play for." If you ever wondered where Jack's commitment and drive came from, look no further than his own father, Kevin. He was in the building trade as a plasterer, one of the toughest jobs around, so he must have instilled the work ethic into his son, and looking at Jack today, you can see that is a fact; Jack never stops running and his attitude is always to fight and win. Kevin is, therefore, fully qualified to recognise his own son's work ethic ever since he put on that Highgate United shirt at the age of six. Jack's father spoke to the Birmingham Mail about his son, "When Jack was 12 or 13 he got in the car and said, 'Dad, do you want to see how good I am?' I didn't think anything more of it. But when Jack showed me what he was doing with his left foot it made me think I should try plastering with my left hand and I thought, 'I've got to work on this!" Kevin puts everything Jack has achieved down to sheer hard work, "He keeps doing extra sessions and his own upper body strength is amazing."

According to Bryan Jones, former Aston Villa Academy Director, he knew right away that Jack had something extra about him, even at the age of nine years old, but he wasn't sure whether it would develop into 'the real thing'; usually academy coaches don't pick players out until they start senior school, but Jack was different. At the age of 12 or 13, coaches usually have some idea of their talent and if they will progress and kick on, but it was that special 'something' that immediately stood Jack out from the crowd; everyone knew that Jack Grealish was destined to play at the top level.

I guess being an academy coach is a difficult job, especially when it involves nine-year-old kids; saying someone won't make it at such a tender age must be heart-breaking for the kid, the parents and the coach; however, the Villa coaches didn't have that conversation with the Grealish family. Young academy lads are encouraged to enjoy their experience; for most kids, it is an experience if nothing else, as most don't make it to the big time for whatever reason, but for the Jack Grealish's of the world, the world is their oyster, or it could be if they kick on from their raw potential. If they are lucky enough to catch the eye of the coaches, the kids and their parents are pulled to one side to see if they are interested in signing for the club. Maybe nine years of age is too young to tell a kid he's got a special talent, but that's the system nowadays; it didn't hurt Jack Grealish one little bit. There's a reason why special kids get signed so early – someone else will sign them if you don't. Aston Villa were lucky enough to sign Jack as a nine-year-old. Not that he would have gone elsewhere if they hadn't, seen as Jack and his family were all Villa fans.

The academy system in England has evolved over the years and kids are now encouraged to let their flair develop if they have that talent. In Jack's case, he always liked to skip past one, two or three defenders, and still to this day he does that with ease. As a nine-year-old he was allowed to play that way because that was his style and it was encouraged. Kids are more likely to develop if they are encouraged to play their natural game; Jack was no exception and the coaches allowed him to show what he was made of. Maybe that wasn't 'coaching' in the true sense of the word, but it seemed to be the right tact to develop his natural ability and allow it to flow.

Schools these days are well equipped to cater for the rare talent that sometimes appears and Jack's school were good enough to realise that he would be away from school from time-to-time, training with the Villa Academy and as long as it didn't affect his education, they made allowances for him, which was only right, given he had so much talent as a footballer; in Jack's case, it didn't have an adverse effect on his schooling. By the time he was 15, Jack had left school and was being educated at the Bodymoor Heath training ground, which at the time was going through a redevelopment. His father, Kevin told the Birmingham Mail, "He was just football, football, football. He'd go at it hell for leather and really worked hard. He wasn't the biggest lad at that time, around average height, but he was playing against kids who were two years or more older than himself. He pushed himself through the age groups and although there's always an influx of talent coming and going at every football club in the country, Jack was the one Villa wanted to keep hold of at all costs."

According to Bryan Jones, Jack was playing wide on the left and he was skipping past players, cutting inside and running into the box as if the defenders were invisible, just as he does now. The coaches were amazed at his skill and close control while ghosting past people, he tended to suck players in. It's not that Jack is, or ever has been, an ultra-quick player, far from it, but he just looks faster than he actually is, by the way he glides past people. It's another talent that can't be coached. At that age, the coaches knew they had a very intelligent player on their hands.

That intelligence extended to him being fouled a lot. That part of the game can't be coached; maybe you call it being clever or shear willingness to win a foul, it's something that has stayed in his game. One of Jack's academy pals, Lewis Kinsella spoke about Jack in the Birmingham Mail, "As a kid he could trick his way past people but would get clipped and win free-kicks. We'd have to kick him sometimes to stop him, not deliberately, it was just you couldn't get near him. He'd get properly upset." Speaking about him going to ground easily, his father said, "People say he goes down too easily, but he draws it with the ball three or four inches in front of his foot and a football brain that's three or four seconds ahead of everybody else. Passes, intricate things, that's how he gets the fouls. I keep telling him to take kicks quick before people get into position."

Around that time, the likes of Gabby Agbonlahor and Gareth Barry were the star names at Villa Park, and Jack couldn't believe his luck that he was in and around those guys. At the end of every season, the first-team players would give their match balls away to the youngsters and Jack managed to get one and was absolutely fascinated with it, according to his father; he'd take it everywhere with him, "He just couldn't believe the first team players like Gabby or Gareth Barry kicked that ball he had in his garden. He thought it was mad."

One thing that most people don't realise is that the coaches were very disciplined towards the academy players at the Villa training ground. The regime under Kevin MacDonald and Tony McAndrew in particular was very strict. However, according to former Lewis Kinsella, they had a very good upbringing, albeit disciplined, "You don't realise how great it is and how big a club (Villa) it is until you're not there. It's a great grounding. We had to clean boots. I had to clean Charles N'Zogbia and Gabby's (Agbonlahor). We'd have to do jobs around the training ground and I remember we had to roll the pitch covers over the pitch at Villa Park when it was snowing. I think there was a rule that you couldn't wear coloured boots until you'd made your first team debut, so Jack had to abide by that."

At the age of 15 Jack stayed in digs in the Walmley area of Sutton Coldfield, north of Birmingham and close enough to both Bodymoor Heath and Villa Park. It was normal that there were two youth team players staying in the same house and they were very well looked after. It was a way of teaching the kids to grow up quickly and be independent. His father spoke of Jack's experience as a youth team player to the Birmingham Mail, "What would happen is the lads would have to walk to Sutton (Coldfield) and they'd get picked up and dropped off there and they'd have to find their own way around. It wasn't Solihull so Jack had to learn. He still speaks to some of the Irish lads who were part of that youth team: Mickey Drennan, Graham Burke and Enda Stevens (he's now at Sheffield United). He loved the Irish lads and still makes time for absolutely everyone. I can't imagine him getting away walking around Sutton now, though, he'd be mobbed!"

Jack was interviewed on the Aston Villa website in March 2021 and spoke about his dreams and aspirations for being a footballer and he suggested that it wasn't until he was around 13 or 14 years old that he realised he could make a living out of the game he absolutely loved and he could become a professional footballer, and a top one at that.

Chapter 3

RIPPING UP THE 'L' PLATES

A season-long loan to Notts County was just the ticket for the teenager.

The European NextGen Series of 2012 – 2013 was a big deal for 17-year-old Jack Grealish of Aston Villa. It was the European Champions League for Under-19s, with clubs like Inter Milan, Liverpool, Dortmund, PSV, Ajax, Chelsea, Juventus, PSG, Manchester City and Barcelona to name but a few involved in the biggest youth cup in European football.

Paul Lambert was Villa's first-team manager at the time, and he was in the stands at the Stadio Giuseppe Sinigaglia in Como, Italy, to watch Jack and his fellow Villans beat Chelsea Under-19s by 2 – 0 in the final, with Graham Burke grabbing a brace for Villa. The relatively unknown figure of Jack Grealish impressed for the team in claret and blue and was one of the stand-out performers on the night, with his silky attacking talent dazzling throughout the series and again in the final.

The raw talent was there for everyone to see. That was the platform Jack Grealish had craved for since the age of nine, to be a winner in a final, be it an Under-19 competition. With the eyes of the first-team manager watching his every move and probably lots of scouts, too - it was just the opportunity he needed to push for a first-team place. The 17-year-old told AVTV, "That was probably one of my favourite times of my short career. Playing for Villa in the NextGen, going abroad and obviously winning it."

After collecting his medal in that final, and producing a stunning performance, Jack's career was meant to immediately take off to the next level, but it didn't exactly work out that way. Instead, he was shipped out to bottom of League One club, Notts County, initially for three months until 13th January 2014 "to gain first team experience."

At the time, Jack was 'highly-rated' at Villa and had been involved in several first-team pre-season friendlies, making his senior debut in the draw at Wycombe and scoring his first senior goal at Walsall. He showed promise but obviously not enough for Paul Lambert to take a chance on him.

One thing that got in the way at Villa seemed to be the manager at the time, Paul Lambert. He told beIN Sports that he and Jack didn't always see eye-to-eye during the early days of his Aston Villa career, when he was first introduced into the first-team fold, "I had Jack as a young kid and we gave him his debut. We put him on the bench and threw him on when he was a kid. Like any other young kid, you have your fall outs and things like that because you're trying to put him on the right path. And like any young kid, they have their pals and different distractions." In that interview, Lambert spoke about managing a young, up-and-coming Jack, with the pitfalls of nightclubs, alcohol and girls as the main 'distractions'.

It could be said the media pay too much attention to footballers. Just because he was in the spotlight doesn't mean he won't make mistakes – everyone makes mistakes and regret certain things they've done. Footballers are no different to anyone else, other than they get paid a lot more, but that shouldn't come into it. Unfortunately, it does. While I don't want to dwell on Jack's private life, there has been some negative publicity surrounding Jack Grealish in the national media in the past, especially when he was very young, some of it probably was of his own doing, some of it unsolicited for sure. If you consider some of the early reports published. The media were getting worked up about his behaviour; however, he was a young lad growing up like any other 19 or 20-year-old, but in the 21st century media, and more importantly, social media, there isn't any room for footballers misbehaving anymore. Everything is noticed, scrutinised and interpreted (or mis-interpreted) – and tenfold.

A lot of lads that age like going out drinking and having a good time, and there's nothing wrong with that in essence, and Jack probably was no different at that age. As Leigh Curtis, the Notts County writer for the Nottingham Post said, "The problem with football is that we set such a high bar for professional footballers we forget at the end of the day, they are just human beings. We make far too much of what they get up to. As long as they aren't breaking any laws or getting into fights, then leave them to it."

These days people in the spotlight can't get away with anything because most people have cameras on their phones and all is recorded and downloaded onto social media. It's part of modern-day life, like it or not. Even though kids these days see professional footballers as 'role models' there's no code that they have to adhere to; they are just like anyone else who is finding their own way in life. Unfortunately, cheap headlines can cause significant damage to people's lives, so young footballers have to learn from their experiences.

Season 2013 – 2014

So, with the 2013 – 2014 season underway, Jack was left in limbo, thinking he'd done enough to earn a first-team place, but Paul Lambert thought otherwise.

The season started brilliantly for Villa, winning away at the new Emirates stadium, who were the first team to win there and they won convincingly, 3 – 1; however, Jack was nowhere near the squad.

Just after the international break in September, Jack signed on loan for Notts County and suddenly, Nottingham seemed like a good place to be after all.

At the age of 18 years and four days, Jack made his debut for his loan club, Notts County in the 59th minute, wearing the number 7 shirt, away to MK Dons on 14th September 2013. Although the result didn't go the Magpies' way (they lost 3 – 1), it effectively spelt the beginning of Jack Grealish's professional football career. On the opposing bench was a one, Dele Alli, who was making a name for himself in the MK Dons side at the time.

"It'll be a good experience" and "he'll come back a better player" are the usual terms used by managers when a young starlet goes out on loan to a smaller club or to a lower league club. The assumption normally is that the player will come back and slot right into the first team, but for Jack Grealish that wasn't the assumption and it wasn't the case in the end either. Jack hadn't even made his first-team debut for Villa by the middle of September 2013. He was sent out on loan to Notts County and few people had not even heard of him, let alone seen him play; maybe only the die-hard Villa supporters who followed the Under-23s or had been to the pre-season friendlies. Yes, he had started to show signs of genius in the youth set-up, but it would have been wishful thinking to see him as a world-beater at the age of 18.

Clubs like Notts County rely on loanees from the bigger clubs; players like Jack, who show potential and just need some confidence and games under their belt at senior level. Those players who don't fit into their team selection or formation are farmed out, whilst players who the fans had written off just drift into obscurity. However, for some, it's a positive step up and a chance to shine - that's just how Jack Grealish saw the opportunity playing for Notts County. It's only natural for football fans of the lower league clubs or smaller clubs to be sceptical of loanees because a lot of them go back to their parent clubs and are never seen or heard of again – that's a damn shame and another story entirely.

League One was very different from the spotlight of the Premier League; some would say it's a harder and more demanding league, so for Jack, it would have proved a huge challenge, and one he would have relished. Although loan moves are normally a gamble, and young players sent out to lower league clubs always have 'potential', there's also an amount of luck involved. No loan move comes with any guarantees, so it's up to the player to apply himself and work hard, then the rewards should come later in his career, but Jack didn't need any of that, because he had something special – he had the 'X-Factor'.

The County manager at the time, Chris Kiwomya, initially signed Jack from Villa, but within a couple of months, Jack was contending with a change of manager, and in came Shaun Derry on 6th November.

Kiwomya had played Jack as an inside number 10, together with Callum McGregor, who was also on loan (from Celtic). McGregor struck up a vital partnership with Jack during their time at County, "I got there just before Jack did," McGregor told The Glasgow Times, "Chris Kiwomya had a really good, technical team. He liked to play Jack and I as inside Number 10s, and I would cut in from the right. From day one, you could see that Jack had a lot of potential. He would dribble past people as if he just jogging. He has that God-given talent where he just glides beyond defenders and we all expected him to have a great career. I felt he would become a top player and you can see him maturing for Villa and becoming a real talisman. It was about Jack progressing as a player and a character, but I'm not surprised at his success. We were a good football team, and we scored a lot of goals. The problem was that we would score four and let in five. We just couldn't defend but I loved the experience. I was a kid and early on you feel like you have no responsibility on the pitch. I would get the ball, shoot and try to score. But you soon learn you are playing with men and scoring two goals in a 4 - 2 defeat isn't 90 minutes' work. You have to go through all those building processes to come of age as a player and realise what is really important."

The first time Leigh Curtis saw Jack play, he knew he was 'special' and it was evident from his first appearance in the black and white stripes that he'd make it in the Premier League later in his career. Jack was given a role by County manager, Shaun Derry in a left-sided position, where he would be able to play his natural game, which was to drop his shoulder, cut inside and try his luck on goal, or unselfishly pass to one of his team-mates. Even though his game has progressed since, his style hasn't and he's just got better and better. Curtis commented further, "He's got all the skills, but what I liked about him most was, when he got kicked or had lumps taken out of him it didn't bother him; he'd pick himself up and kept going again. He was such a delight to watch; he was one of those players you just loved to watch because he gets bums off seats. He was very skilful, scored some great goals and was a really nice lad off the pitch. You can tell from talking to the people in and around the club, that they all knew he was going to go on to be destined for bigger and better things. He had that boyish excitement in him, and sometimes you don't see that from players, but you really had it with Jack. There aren't many players around with his ability. He may not be the quickest, but the way he controls the ball, the way he spots a pass or the way he creates openings, he really is a fantastic talent. The scary thing is he's only going to get better. Players don't normally reach their full development until they are 26 or 27 so it's absolutely frightening how good he is now and how good he could be in the next few years."

Watching at close quarters this developing talent perform for Notts County, week in, week out, was like "watching an artist in the last phase of a masterpiece," according to Curtis. "A slight touch here, a little flick there."

In the game against Gillingham on 7th December 2013, Jack scored his first senior goal (and his first for County) in the 87th minute - and what a goal it was. A solo effort, beating three Gillingham defenders along the way to finish off with a powerful shot into the roof of the net. It was good enough to win the December Goal of the Month competition for League One. Curtis described the goal in the Nottingham Post, "Then came the glorious finale. He shimmied past the first challenge, drove past the second and danced past the third. Their defenders scrambled to stop Jack, but the outcome was inevitable – Jack scored, to the delight of the County faithful, and ran off, with socks rolled down to celebrate with his father. It was an unforgettable goal and everyone who celebrated inside the Meadow Lane stadium was treated to their first glimpse of his raw talent."

Shaun Derry said that Jack was very much a family person and that goal against Gillingham was his favourite memory of working with him, "That was my favourite memory of Jack because it encapsulated everything he is about both as a player and a person. First of all, the goal he scored was above the level we were at, which was League One. When you look back at it, it was unbelievable. There was the double shimmy, taking his man on the outside and he finishes magnificently. But he then goes all the way around Meadow Lane to celebrate; he raced into the stands to hug his dad and I remember him getting booked for it."

Once Jack had recorded his first goal in the latter stages of that game against Gillingham, he quickly got back onto the scoresheet in the next game away to Colchester, as the Magpies recorded back-to-back victories. Jack fired past the Colchester 'keeper on the half-hour and made another contribution in the final minute of time, when he set up Garry Liddle to make it 4 – 0 to County. Derry continued to talk about Jack with excitement, "There were so many outstanding memories of managing Jack throughout that season, but that was the one (his goal against Gillingham). It was not just about the brilliance of what he had just done on the pitch, but it was then having the humility of who he wanted to share it with. When we went in after the game, I said 'do you know what, it was just like watching a little boy who wanted his dad'. He didn't want the rest of the players. He wanted the people who helped him reach the levels of where he had got to and, for me, that tells you everything."

On New Year's Day 2014, Jack scored his third goal for County in a 3 – 0 victory at home to Bradford, a victory which helped the Magpies move off the bottom of the table. Jack's major contributions to the game came late on, very late in fact, in the 88th minute. He combined with Campbell-Ryce to set up Callum McGregor score the second goal, then one minute into injury time, Jack got on the score sheet himself when he slotted in the third.

It was only just the start of the emerging talent that we all know now, a talent the whole world has now come to finally embrace. It was just the start of Jack's massive contribution to Notts County's season when his feet were moving around like a hypnotist's pendulum.

For those people who witnessed day in, day out, the coaches and players on the training ground, it was just another day at the office (or the training ground). Former club captain, Alan Sheehan took young Jack under his wing and they quickly formed a strong bond, on and off the pitch according to Leigh Curtis. It quickly became apparent to Sheehan, and to everyone at County, that he wasn't just another 18-year-old footballer brought in from a big club to get 'experience'. Sheehan told Leigh Curtis that Jack was "something else" and a very special talent, and the words were heart-felt indeed, "When he came in, obviously none of us knew much about him," says Sheehan. "But I remember we were training at Highfields (Notts County training ground) and, at the time, we had to drive down there in our kit because there were no changing rooms. And as soon as I saw him there, it was his physique that immediately hit you. He was wearing these Nike boots; he was given the ball and then he started dribbling. I thought 'wow' this guy moves and plays differently from anything I'd ever seen. It was effortless and there were some days in training when, as a defender, it was just painful. You would be like 'stay away from me today, please'. In one of his first games, I am stood there watching him just glide past defenders, experienced ones too. There was no fear. Nothing fazed him. Just give him the ball and off he went. At that point, I knew this kid was the real deal. For a large amount of that season, we played down the left-hand side together and we struck up this wonderful relationship. Every time I had the ball, he was the first pass I looked for. I'd give it to him; teams would double up and sometimes he would take the two of them on. If not, he laid it back to me and I put the ball in the box. It was quite simple back then because that's the way we played most of the time. But honestly, man, I loved him. I loved everything about him. The way he carried himself on and off the pitch was always confident but never arrogant."

As Leigh Curtis previously suggested, he wasn't the quickest player on the park, but he saw a yard or two in his head, so he was already a yard or two quicker than anyone else because of what he saw, "He had a wonderful balance about him; some players look a bit clunky, but he glides along and has full control of the ball. He's a magician, really." Leigh Curtis said he was very fortunate to have seen someone like Jack play for Notts County during that season, "It was a high-pressured situation, Notts County were fighting it out at the bottom and had struggled during that season so that's quite a big ask of an 18-year-old to come in and be able to perform to such a standard. A lot of the fans, knowing how good he was, must have put a lot of pressure on him to perform, week in, week out. I don't think he got enough credit for that, personally. Jack came in, trusted in his own ability, confident in his own skills, and obviously transmitted it on to the pitch. Not once did I think he would get swamped by the pressures of needing to get a win at the weekend, and that's what really impressed me."

During that season, there were times when Jack was 'roughed up' and brushed off the ball, as all the better players are in that league, but Jack was so technically good that it didn't seem to matter to him. His build had changed from the time he was at school to the time he finished his spell at Notts County; he had shot up in height, and later in his career, he has subsequently worked on his physique. Maybe that helped him adapt to the roughness of League One? The swagger with which he played made him the victim of rough treatment from many teams during the season. The experienced players in League One didn't take too kindly to being embarrassed by a teenager and, behind the scenes, Shaun Derry and the Notts County backroom staff were concerned he was being deliberately targeted. However, Jack was so good and so important to the cause he became almost un-droppable.

With his loan spell coming to an end, and his Villa career in doubt, Jack announced on Twitter that he was staying with the Magpies for the rest of the season. It wasn't always certain whether he'd stay at County or find another loan club. However, his Tweet spelt it out:

"I thank other League [One] and Championship clubs for the interest but at the moment Notts County is the best place for my development."

County then announced the deal on their website on Thursday 16th January 2014:

"Notts County are delighted to announce that Aston Villa winger Jack Grealish has agreed new loan deal with the club until the end of the season. The club would like to thank Aston Villa for allowing Jack to re-join the Magpies and for the professional and efficient manner in which they have handled discussions over the loan deal."

Leigh Curtis remembered a particular game at Stevenage on 18th January 2014 when Notts County won 1 – 0 and he was absolutely brilliant, but unfortunately, he was lampooned by a Stevenage defender which left the backroom staff watching through splayed fingers, and later Jack needed to be substituted due to the injury he sustained as a result. Later on, tempers snapped in the dugout and Derry flew into a rage with his opposite number.

After that game, the County backroom staff were so incensed by what they had seen, they were ready to exchange punches rather than post-match pleasantries. Shaun Derry even refused to have a drink with the opposing manager and turned the jubilation of their 1 - 0 win into bitterness over the rough treatment Jack had endured and the injury he incurred, "Shaun and myself were ready to knock a few people out after that game," recalls former assistant manager, Greg Abbott, who also highlighted the fact that Jack was targeted throughout the latter part of the season as well, "During that season, some of the treatment Jack was subjected to really became a concern. I've fought all my life to be competitive, but there was always fairness with me. There were some who wanted to kick him off the park, but to want to do that to an 18-year-old is not quite right."

If Derry wasn't incensed enough, his further comments following that Stevenage game summed up his mood, "Teams were being clever. One player hits him. Then another. Then another. It's really disappointing. We haven't got enough talent in this country for players like Jack to be subjected to the treatment he had to endure. It was almost a case of look 'we've got to stop Jack at all costs' and that wasn't right. After that Stevenage game, we had to put our arm around him and made sure he was okay because he could have quite easily thought 'do you know what? This isn't for me this.' We just reassured him that he had to take it as a compliment. Of course, you understand there is a competitive edge, but there is a line that shouldn't be crossed. But he dealt with that brilliantly. He got back into the team very quickly and was soon back playing well for us again."

Shaun Derry must have been a happy man, having such a talented player on his hands, at least for one season. However, I'm sure he'll look back on that spell and realise how much of a part he played in Jack's development. There aren't too many of those type players around these days; coaching tends to take away the rawness that most players begin their career with, but Curtis remembered those days with fondness, "I liked him because he was like one of those players in a playground who took the ball and ran at people."

For Jack, he knew it was a pressured situation he found himself in, and he knew people were watching him; scouts from Villa and other clubs, so he must have been aware of the spotlight he was in, even though, and no disrespect to Notts County, he was only playing at a club at the bottom of League One. Having said that, he most certainly contributed to Notts County's season, with some important goals and assists, and that's testament to him as a person and a player. It would have been all too easy for Jack to gone into his shell and not care about the situation, which is what some young players may have done, given the same scenario.

Jack played a seismic role as Derry's side hit promotion form in the final run of games and in the penultimate fixture of the season, a 2 - 0 victory over Swindon Town at Meadow Lane on 26th April, according to Curtis, he was "simply unplayable". The Magpies took an early lead when Alan Sheehan received the ball with a cut-back from Jack and rifled in a shot from the edge of the box on 9 minutes. Callum McGregor finished it off with a 99th minute goal, shortly after a double sending off involving two Swindon players. Jack had made an enormous contribution to that game which left County two places above the relegation zone.

On the last day of the season, County only needed a positive result to survive when they played at Oldham and they came from behind to snatch a 1 - 1 draw courtesy of an Alan Sheehan equalising penalty in the 75th minute. The result left County one place and three points above the relegation zone. At the final whistle, more than 3,000 fans, some of whom came in fancy dress, stormed onto the pitch and hoisted Jack onto their shoulders and worshipped him like a God. What those fans didn't realise though, was the pressure on Jack to perform in that game, "Jack was magnificent for us in that season, but I will tell you the day it finally got on top of him and it was Oldham," Greg Abbott told Leigh Curtis that Jack sometimes needed to be kept in check and not think he can bomb forward at every opportunity. "This story isn't out there in the open, but it was so tense given what was at stake. Thousands of fans had travelled and I'll never forget what the away end looked like that day. There was this sea of black and white and you're carrying all their hopes and expectations. Naturally, there is a great deal of pressure attached to that because you've got all these people relying on you to make sure everything goes to plan. But during the first half, Jack was told in no uncertain terms that he needed to do this, needed to do that, he needed to track back and make tackles. It really upset him so in that 15-minute break at half-time, I had to do a real man-management job on him. I had to get him to come round, make him realise just how big of a player he was for us and make him understand just how big of a day it was for the club. Up until that point, he just wasn't getting it. He just wanted to get the ball and play. That's how much out of his depth he was in terms of his age and experience."

That was probably the biggest game Jack had played in up until that day and the season-long loan spell at Notts County turned out to be a huge success for Jack, and for the Magpies. Not only did Jack make a massive difference to the team, but he helped County to one of the greatest escapes in the club's history and kept their League One status for one more season at least. It could be said that they wouldn't have managed it without Jack. Greg Abbott continued, "I guess Jack would say he probably learned a lot from it but I will tell you, it was one of the longest 15 minutes I've ever had during my career (during last 15 minutes of the Oldham game). The simple fact is that without Jack, we lose the game, no question about it. We needed everybody at their best. But he came out for the second half and played a major part in getting that result. But I've got to be honest, at one point, I thought the importance of the day, what was riding on it, was just going to be too much for him. That day was a big occasion for Notts County and Jack will go through it time and again in his career, because he will play in cup finals, he will play for England and he will play for a team aiming to win the league. But that day wasn't easy for him and I am sure he will admit that."

Shaun Derry said he was proud to have worked with Jack throughout that season and described him as "a dream to manage on and off the pitch at Meadow Lane. He single-handedly won games for us, whether he scored the goals, whether he created the goals, or whether he occupied two, three and four men in the area that left spaces for others to go and win the game for us. When you think of how young he was, to do that was exceptional. His dad, Kevin used to spend a lot of time at the training ground to see how he was getting on and I spent hours talking to him about his son. He absolutely backs him to the hilt. As he was such a young player, if there were any real problems that I felt that I should not be sorting out, I just handed it over to his dad."

However, Derry recalled the one time his patience was tested before a game against Port Vale on Boxing Day. Having had Christmas Day off and told to reconvene at a nearby hotel before the game, Derry was surprised when Jack walked through the door without his club tracksuit on. "I had given the lads Christmas Day off and we had agreed to meet at the hotel for pre-match. So, we're sitting there and he arrived in a pair of jeans, white trainers and a leather jacket. It wasn't the club tracksuit I remember. I just thought to myself, what was his Christmas Day like because it must have been a little bit different to mine. There's me focusing on the game and Jack just turned up in this outfit that you'd wear to a nightclub. I said to Greg (Abbott), 'he's got a leather jacket on, where's he been?' He (Greg Abbott) gave me this look and said, 'just leave it'. Steam was coming out of my ears. But he's our best player, what do you do when you're struggling? We were fighting for our lives at the bottom of the table and also fighting for our careers. I wanted to be a success at Notts County because it was my first job in management, but you quickly realise you can't do it on your own as a coach or as a manager. You need everybody. But what do you do? Do you get angry? Or do you actually just understand that a young player is going to make some pretty poor decisions at certain times? And that was one for Jack and it was one I overlooked. But I got him on the pitch for the game and pulled him in a couple of days later when the time was right. But I had a good rapport with Jack. I used to tell him all the time that he was the best player in the league, and he was, even at that age."
If that was the only misdemeanour then his behaviour during the loan spell must have been pretty impeccable for the rest of the time.

Derry's fondness towards Jack is plain to see and in a more recent interview, his kind words seem heartfelt indeed, "It gives me an immense proudness of having been able to get to know Jack personally and he absolutely loves his family. People go on about some of the misdemeanours that he has committed off the pitch and he has - they're historic things that he will never be able to change. But deep down he is such a good guy. He sent a wonderful message to my son, Jesse, who absolutely adores him by the way - he's even got the crap 'barnet'. It was a lovely message about football along the lines of always make sure you enjoy the game. Jack still plays like that as a 26-year-old. He loves it. It was a beautiful message and I'll never forget that."

Recalling the time he spent at Notts County, Jack told Footy Talk in March 2021, "I wasn't meant to go on loan that year. I had a little bit of a falling out with the manager at the time which was Paul Lambert and I just got sent to Notts County, who were bottom of League One. Looking back now, it was just the best thing I've ever done. I was playing men's' football week in, week out; it was way different to what you're playing here (at Villa). You had people fighting for their lives, trying to pay their mortgage off every week and it's the real world down there. I absolutely loved it. I'll always have a soft spot for Notts County in my heart. Any advice I could give to a young lad now would be not to try and hang around and play reserve team football, if you can get yourself out there go out on loan, because it helped me so, so much."

Jack also spoke to AVTV about his time on loan, "I went out on loan early and tried to get as much game time as possible; I think I played about 36 or 37 games at Notts County (he played 38) and it set me well on my way."

****

After the eventful season-long loan spell at Notts County, where he appeared 38 times either as a substitute or in the starting line-up, scored five times with seven assists and booked nine times, his Villa manager, Paul Lambert challenged Jack to force his way into the first team for the 2014 – 2015 Premier League season. However, with the League One season finished, he went back to Villa and made his Premier League debut at the back-end of the 2013 – 2014 campaign, with a solitary substitutes' appearance, in the penultimate game of the season, away to Manchester City, when he replaced Ryan Bertrand in the 88th minute. It didn't seem like the right thing to do, bringing him on with Villa at 2 – 0 down with two minutes of the 90 to go, only to see another two goals go in while he was on the pitch. Two minutes plus some injury time was Jack's lot for Villa that season.

Jack had to wait until the following August to get his chance again.

It wasn't as if Villa were doing well in the Premier League – they finished 15th and Lambert told BBC Sport, "He's got a lot of big players in front of him but he's got to try to get in that group. He's a young kid who's still learning the ropes but he's done his chance no harm."

In May 2014, after the season ended, Jack played in the Hong Kong Soccer Sevens, and finished as top scorer with six goals as Villa won the Shield title. With his contract due to expire in the summer of 2015, he was offered a new four-year deal by the club in September 2014 and, although it was touch and go, he eventually signed it on 14th October 2014.

That small bit of faith Lambert had in Jack was shown by his inclusion in the squad that flew to the United States for their pre-season tour and his inclusion in several friendlies. He scored in the game against Chesterfield, "He's done really well on the tour. He didn't disgrace himself and more than held his own." That was some praise indeed from the ever-stubborn Lambert.

Chapter 4

FINDING HIS FEET

How the Villa takeover and a managerial merry-go-round worked in Jack's favour.

Season 2014 – 2015

Jack's hard work during the pre-season was rewarded with a substitutes' appearance in Villa's opening game, an away win at Stoke, when he came on in the 71st minute for Charles N'Zogbia. He was then given his first-team debut in the Capital One League Cup tie at Villa Park against Leyton Orient 11 days later, an embarrassing 1 – 0 defeat, but at least jack got 90 minutes under his belt.

It was not until the FA Cup Third Round tie against Blackpool at Villa Park on 4th January 2015 that Jack made his next full appearance, after half a dozen or so spells coming off the bench in the Premier League. By now, Jack was 19 years-old and he hadn't made a Premier League start yet; he wasn't happy and he made it known to Paul Lambert and the fans. He wanted to play football; he wanted to be happy at a club who wanted him to play a full part in the team, not a bit-part, coming off the bench occasionally. Lambert took exception to his antics and was dropped from the first-team squad – Jack had to train with the Under-21s.

Both Bodymoor Heath, the club's training ground and Villa Park weren't happy places to be. The club's American owner at the time, Randy Lerner wanted out and appeared to be a hands' off CEO, managing the club from 6,000 miles away. Paul Lambert was under pressure, following a string of 10 league games without a win. The Villa fans had been calling for his head for most of the season, calling Lambert's style of football "boring", "negative" or "predictable" - or all three. Then on 11th February 2015, Paul Lambert was inevitably sacked as Villa manager after an embarrassing 2 – 0 defeat at Hull.

To be fair to Lambert after a promising start to his Villa tenuership, he ended up having to work on a tight budget and with the pressure of a disinterested Randy Lerner pulling the plug on high-profile signings when investment in the squad was needed. However, it was the owner's lack of communication with Lambert that added further strain and it eventually wore him down and out of the door.

Where did that leave Jack? Happy, maybe? Afterall, Paul Lambert wasn't exactly 'Mr Popular' with the players – or the long-suffering fans.

Enter Tim Sherwood.

First Team Coach, Scott Marshall took charge for one game, an FA Cup tie at home to Leicester City, before Tim Sherwood was appointed three days after the sacking of Lambert. Tim sat in the stands watching his new team put on a brilliant performance to beat their local rivals, and even gave the half-time team-talk. Jack took his usual place on the bench and came on with seven minutes to go. However, it wasn't a secret that Tim Sherwood was an admirer of Jack, and of youth in general, so his appointment was seen by some (if not most) of the Villa faithful as a good move, at least initially, Sherwood was certainly seen by the board as the standout candidate.

Sherwood was given a three-year contract, and a reported £2m a year, something that was frowned upon by some, but seen as a step in the right direction by others. Sure, he was a high-profile name and fiercely ambitious, but he'd only had less than six months of football management at Spurs following the sacking of André Villas-Boas. However, that didn't detract Villa CEO Tom Fox, who was confident that his arrival would breathe new life into the side, who were struggling in the bottom three. He was given licence to revive their fortunes and to secure Premier League status, even though he had limited experience.

Tim Sherwood's mandate was simple – he had 13 games to save Villa from the drop. "It is a great honour to manage one of the biggest clubs in English football," Sherwood said in a statement on Villa's website, "I can't wait to get started and I'm really looking forward to the challenge."

Sherwood knew of Jack's talent and immediately vowed to take him under his wing and make him a better player. Jack felt isolated under Lambert and hadn't started a League game all season before the manager's sacking. It was time for Jack to show his new boss what he had to offer. "He's got potential," Sherwood told the Aston Villa website, "He needs to fulfil that. I have told him that. I have a track record of developing players and Jack is going to be taken under my wing and I am going to point him in the right direction. He just needs to listen and he will be fine."

Sherwood's reign as Villa manager started just as Lambert's ended, with a defeat (to Stoke). 'Rome wasn't built in a day', or even two. Villa also lost the next game too (against Newcastle).

Sherwood's first win as Villa manager came against West Bromwich Albion in the league on the 3rd March, but he still hadn't given Jack a run out. However, four days later, Jack came on as a 74th minute substitute for Charles N'Zogbia in the FA Cup quarter-final against West Bromwich Albion at a packed Villa Park, with the home side 1 – 0 up through Fabian Delph. Jack's impact was immediate, as he set-up Scott Sinclair for Villa's second goal in the 85th minute, but his cameo appearance on the pitch only lasted a mere 15 minutes. Jack was given his marching orders by referee Anthony Taylor after a second yellow card for diving. It was his first red card of his senior career.

It was around this time that there was talk of whether Jack would prefer to play for England or Ireland; he'd already represented Ireland at under-17, under-19 and under-21 level but was left undecided who he would chose at senior level. There was a massive amount of hype around the subject over the previous few months, but due to his lack of game-time for Villa, a lot of that noise had died down. Sherwood had made suggestions in the media that Jack would choose England over Ireland, "I think he might play for England but he's got to play for Villa first," Sherwood told the Birmingham Mail. It came across that Sherwood had asked Jack if he was more Irish or English, when he assessed his senior international options. Sherwood was keen for the youngster to establish himself in the Premier League before he committed to wearing green of Ireland or the white and blue of England. He told Goal.com, "Jack has to play a few more times for Aston Villa before he needs to make that decision. It's up to Jack where he wants to go. What I've got to do is make sure he's got that decision to make. He must be doing something right for Aston Villa if he's got those options. That's my priority. Then it's up to Jack to decide where he wants to go."

It was another month before Jack was again considered for the first-team, but this time, after 11 substitute appearances for the club that season, he made the starting line-up for the first time in the Premier League in the 3 – 3 draw at home to Queens Park Rangers on 7th April. However, he was replaced by Joe Cole after 70 minutes. Playing in a left-side of midfield role, it was an important game for Jack, who was eager to impress his manager – and he didn't disappoint.

It was a performance that was applauded, and raised a few eyebrows, but it was a performance that was always coming. I think by that time, everyone who had watched Jack play in his cameo roles knew what a talent he was, maybe with the exception of Paul Lambert?

Jack impressed Tim Sherwood so much, he started the next Premier League game away to Spurs, and what an impact he had. A 35th minute goal by Villa cult hero, Christian Benteke, was enough to give Villa a 1 – 0 win against Sherwood's former club, but Jack only lasted 63 minutes.

Within the space of a couple of months, Tim Sherwood had rejuvenated his Villa side after replacing Paul Lambert, who couldn't get a tune out of the same set of players. Sherwood had the personality and style whereas Lambert didn't, and maybe that was the difference the players saw in him? Something was working in Sherwood's favour, and as for Jack, it seemed he had finally cracked it.

Next up was a FA Cup semi-final tie against Liverpool at Wembley on 24ᵗʰ April 2015. This was to be the biggest game in Jack's career to date, and a chance to star in front of 85,000 fans and millions watching at home. The FA Cup is the biggest and best domestic cup competition in the world, and the most famous, and Jack had a chance to shine at last, and in front of a big audience. With only two senior starts in the Premier League career under his belt, it was a massive game, and it was a big deal for Jack.

Before the two semi-finals took place, the pundits were expecting (and probably hoping) for a 'showpiece final' between Arsenal and Liverpool but Jack and his Villa side had different ideas. In from the start, Jack was a giant on the pitch, who played with a calm that defied his 19 years. It seemed the whole team were calm and relaxed, confident and composed. Ironically, Liverpool went ahead on the half-hour mark through Philippe Coutinho. However, Villa responded in perfect fashion as Fabian Delph played a one-two with Jack before pulling the ball back to Benteke, who side-footed the ball into the bottom corner. Villa continued to press forward after the break and they got their second goal when Benteke's back heel fell into the path of Jack, who instinctively released Delph to cut inside Lovren and fired his shot past Mignolet in the Liverpool goal.

As for Jack, he'd done his job during his 84 minutes he was on the Wembley pitch, and was replaced by Joe Cole, with Villa already 2 – 1 up. It was the least they deserved and Liverpool had no answer to Villa's work-rate; it could have been more, but there were no further goals.

The Villa fans were celebrating at long last.

Villa fan Jack also celebrated that night and in a subsequent interview with The Athletic, he admitted, "I've not said this before, but it was the most emotional I've ever been after a game. I went into the showers on my own and started crying. I was 19, so I was a bit shy. I felt like I had to hide away from my team-mates and let it all out. That feeling, when it had all sunk in, going up to see my mum and dad at Wembley was amazing. They told me that they were so proud of me and I'll never forget that."

Villa's win was a triumph for Tim Sherwood as his side produced a performance of style, composure and grit to reach only their second FA Cup final since 1957, when they beat Manchester United. They were bristling and business-like, in contrast to Brendan Rodgers' talented side who were poor, dismal it could be said, and again, they failed to deliver on the day. Sherwood praised Jack for his performance, saying the bigger the occasion, the better he gets.

'Super Jack' had arrived on the scene!

Following the furore of the FA Cup semi-final victory, Jack started every League game leading up to the Final; in fact, he'd featured in every game since 7th April. Two wins and three defeats was enough to keep Villa safe in the Premier League, with three points and one place separating Villa in 17th from Hull City in 18th place. It was still a dreadful season, but it could have been worse if Tim Sherwood hadn't have come in during February.

Just before the FA Cup Final, it was discovered that Jack's great-great-grandfather was in fact, Billy Garraty who had played for Villa in the 1905 FA Cup Final - it was an amazing coincidence indeed. Apparently, Garraty was man-of-the-match as Villa went on to win their fourth cup final. Jack Grealish had a chance to do the same, 110 years on, "I've got a lot of Villa history in my family; my whole family are Villa fans."

That semi-final victory over Liverpool was soon forgotten on 30th May when the same old familiar Villa turned up at Wembley to face Arsenal, or rather they didn't turn up as they were battered 4 – 0 by Arsène Wenger's side. The manner of defeat seemed to sum up the season. There isn't too much to say about that performance, and Jack summed it up in one word on his Twitter feed after the game, "Gutted!" he said.

****

The first real low point in Jack's career came during the summer break, when an incident occurred while on holiday in Tenerife, where he was photographed laying on a footpath after having a few drinks and hit the national headlines for the wrong reasons. Remember, this was before Jack was even holding down a regular Villa first-team place and went under the national radar somewhat; if you weren't a Villa fan and didn't know his potential, Jack was just another young footballer, "I felt like a kid last summer and in February last year, before Tim Sherwood came in, nobody would have known who I was. I didn't realise what the attention would be like, I just thought I'd go on holiday like all young lads do." It was a harsh reality check for Jack who had quickly become a local hero to thousands of young Villa fans. He told The Telegraph in 2016, "We all make mistakes when we're young but you won't be seeing me do any of that again. I look back on it now and as a professional footballer you can't do that sort of thing. We're supposed to be role models for kids. I feel like I've matured a lot and grown up since then. It's all about learning and I'm still only 20. You can see why the fans got frustrated and I've got a little bit to make up with them." Those words were quite mature for a 20-year-old and his remorse for those actions were plain to see. Tim Sherwood later warned Jack about his behaviour and was quoted as saying, "We all did it. You can't live a normal life unfortunately. You're in the public eye. You're an example. There needs to be a level of self-discipline. He knows what's right and what's wrong."

Despite the mixed-up season Jack encountered, being in and out of the side, he ended up being named Aston Villa Young Player of the Year.

****

Season 2015 – 2016

Having just survived another season in the Premier League, the Villa board kept faith with Tim Sherwood for the start of the new season for the club's 28th consecutive season in the top-flight of English football (24th in the Premier League). Tim Sherwood had given the club an injection of positivity, if nothing else, and he was about to embark on his first pre-season as a manager.

The usual merry-go-round of players coming and going started during the early summer, with key players like Shay Given, Darren Bent, Andreas Weimann and Ron Vlaar being released to the dismay of the Villa faithful, as well as cult hero, Christian Benteke going to Liverpool. Micah Richards became Sherwood's first of 13 new signings, which included not one Jordan, but three in the likes of: Amavi, Ayew and Veretout, all from French clubs. In the July, Fabian Delph performed an amazing U-turn after committing himself to the club one week, only to sign for Manchester City for a miserly £8m the week after, and in that he became a 'hate figure' for Villa fans, who gave him the name of 'snake'. Even more mysteriously, Villa's all-time record goal-scorer, Gabriel Agbonlahor was made club captain after Delph's controversial departure.

All the upheaval and negative headlines set the tone for the season ahead.

Villa started the season well with a brilliant 1 – 0 win away at Bournemouth, and there were positive signs in that game, and that things were changing. Jack scored his first ever Premier League goal in the fifth game of the season, away to Leicester City. Villa were dominant in the first half as they took the lead with his deserved opener. Carles Gil swept in a second early in the second half, but it went downhill soon afterwards as the visitors went down 3 – 2. Four points from five games kept them just above the relegation zone, but only just.

Speaking after a 3 – 2 defeat at Anfield on 26th September, Sherwood heaped praises on Jack, "I wouldn't want to sell Jack Grealish for £60m today put it that way, I know what he could possibly be. What looks expensive this year might not be expensive next year. That's the way the game is going. He's a great player is Jack, but he's got to realise – I've been on at him every day – there is more to the game than just when you're in possession. That Liverpool game was huge with a lot of expectancy and pressure, it didn't faze him, he grew more. He is certainly a type of player we have seen at the very top level for the likes of Liverpool and in the past for Aston Villa, we have to recognise that. He's not a shop window job, he's our player, and we couldn't put a price on him. I certainly wouldn't."

The disastrous set of results continued; Villa returned only four points out of a possible 30. While Sherwood definitely was an advocate of Jack's, featuring in seven out of those 10 games he wasn't a shoo-in for a starring role. After eight (interesting) months in charge of Aston Villa, the board's patience run thin and they relieved Tim Sherwood of his position after a 2 – 1 home defeat against Swansea on 24th October. Sherwood was in charge for 28 games and that was the shortest spell of any permanent Villa manager (up until then).

The season was turning into yet another disaster, on and off the pitch.

Under-21 manager, Kevin MacDonald took temporary charge of the first-team for their trip to White Hart Lane while the board found a replacement and Jack's future was again put into question. Regardless of who came in, Jack would have to start from a clean slate once again.

At that time, Villa Park was a hard place to play, not only for the visiting side, but for the home side; the fans had been a volatile bunch for the previous five or six seasons, since the wheels came off following Martin O'Neill's sudden departure and the financial crisis hit the club. Whoever came in would be managing a club four points from safety and bottom of the table and in disarray.

That man was Rémi Garde, former Lyon and Arsenal defensive midfielder, who had a reputation as a 'tidy and reliable' footballer in his day and was part of the Gunners' double-winning squad of 1997 – 1998. His appointment raised a few eyebrows but didn't spark any jubilations amongst the locals. He'd only managed Lyon for three seasons and had been out of work since May 2014 before being appointed Villa boss on 2nd November 2015. It was hardly an inspiring appointment to say the least. Furthermore, the Villa board gave him a three-and-a-half-year contract, which was even more bizarre.

However, Garde was a well-respected player and a disciplinarian as a coach, something lacking at Villa Park - maybe that was the reason why he was appointed? He described joining the club as an, "unbelievable honour" and told the BBC, "Obviously we have a difficult task in front of us but I'm looking forward to the challenge." It was another risky appointment, none-the-less.

Garde's reign started encouragingly enough as Villa held leaders

Manchester City to a goalless draw at Villa Park and they suddenly found a defensive solidity, not seen since the opening day of the season. However, they were less effective going forward as usual and didn't manage a shot on target. After featuring in most of Sherwood's squad, Jack was named as an unused substitute, with Garde preferring Idrissa Gueye on the left side of midfield for his first game in charge. According to Jack, speaking to AVTV, he said it was a tough time and he "wasn't a proper first team established player, I was just in and out." It wasn't a good start for Jack, trying to impress his talents on the new manager.

There was another low point in Jack's early career that he'd probably want to forget. Following the goalless draw with Manchester City, the next game ended in an abysmal 4 – 0 defeat at Everton two weeks later, and Jack was substituted after 74 minutes. However, it was what happened in the evening that made the headlines, and for the wrong reasons. Jack was captured on video partying in a Manchester night club, late into the Saturday night, following that defeat at Goodison Park. It wasn't the first time off-the-field incidents had hindered Jack's profile. "We'd got well beaten and I still went out, looking back it was stupid. We weren't having a great season and those are the days you've got to go home and reflect on it and stick your head under the pillow," Jack subsequently explained.

Those comments suggest he is far from the stereotypical young footballer disconnected from modern day life. Talking to people who know Jack, he is intelligent and acutely aware how privileged he is to be playing for his hometown club. He is adored by the Villa fans and I'm sure those two incidents didn't dampen their love for him.

Speaking after that defeat at Everton, Garde told the Independent, "Jack is a very gifted player with a lot of skill and quality, but in the last few games he was not at the level he should have been. He is a guy who is always smiling and is a nice person. I don't have a problem with Jack. It is as simple as that. He needed more confidence and more structure in his game." Garde also called Jack an "unfinished player", which was probably a fair assessment at the time.

It was clear Jack was struggling for form with the club at rock-bottom, and now he was facing a fight to prove to new manager, Rémi Garde that he was worthy of a place in the side. However, the Frenchman would not have been impressed by the front-page headlines he'd made. It was also evident that Jack was on a head-on clash with a manager who was desperately trying to assert his authority with a disillusioned squad.

It was a car crash waiting to happen!

The time had come for Jack to knuckle down and concentrate on his football if he was to live up to his talent. He was catching the eye of the media on and off the pitch, but unfortunately, not so much on the pitch.

Apart from having to deal with disciplining Jack, Rémi Garde had a battle on his hands because the club wanted to appoint the highly-rated Steve Round, as first team coach to assist him on the training ground, but Garde claimed there was no room for another coach. After only a few games in charge, it seemed like he had the whole world on his shoulders but he remained positive about his belief Villa were going to stay up, "Probably, elsewhere in the country no one else believes in that. But here at Villa Park and around the club we need to feel that it is still possible. It's very important that we are very focused. Despite the bad result at Everton the fans will still be behind the team."

The supposition that Jack was heading for a showdown with Garde was made fact when he was dropped from the first team squad and had to train with the Under-21s, following that incident in Manchester. He didn't feature for the following two games, a home defeat to Watford and a rare draw with Southampton. However, Jack was re-introduced into the first team as a 78th minute substitute in the home defeat to Arsenal on 13th December.

Even though the performances had improved, the results hadn't, and to add insult to injury, Rémi Garde's team, albeit not all of his doing, had broken some unwanted records. Aston Villa were now without a win in 15 league games - the joint-longest run in English football (along with York), and things weren't going to get any better. The fans, who weren't happy, made their feelings known after that

Arsenal defeat as boos could be heard ringing round Villa Park.

It would not be until after Christmas that Jack was re-introduced into the first team arena, an away trip to fellow-strugglers, Norwich City. Jack came on as an 81st minute substitute for Jordan Veretout with Villa 1 – 0 down and conceding a second late on.

There was a rare start for Jack in the first game of 2016, another defeat, this time away at Sunderland, who themselves were fighting for their Premier League survival. Jack only lasted 57 minutes before being replaced by Adama Traore.

With 20 games played, Garde's side only had eight points on the board, had only scored 16 goals and were 11 points from safety. It was looking grim for Villa. Apart from a couple of bit-parts in FA Cup games in January, Jack later suffered an ankle injury that would keep him out for three months.

By the first week in February, there was a chink of light for Villa as they managed to pick up eight points from five games, but they were still deep in trouble and eight points from safety, but at least they were fighting – albeit without Jack.

Come March 2016, the club were still in all sorts of trouble, both on and off the pitch. The Villa CEO, Tom Fox and Sporting Director, Hendrik Almstadt had both left their posts before the away game at Swansea on 19th March. With the owner, Randy Lerner, still trying to sell the club, the approachable Tom Fox had become a target for the fans' frustration and his role had become untenable. Not only that, it was tough for everyone at the club; players, backroom staff, and also office and matchday staff. There was a lot of depression around the club; people were losing their jobs. It really wasn't a nice place to be.

To make matters worse, Villa suffered another defeat at Swansea.

That defeat also signalled the end of Rémi Garde, after only 147 days at Villa Park. He surpassed Tim Sherwood's unwanted record of being the shortest serving manager in the club's history, adding to the record of having the worst win percentage (10%); he'd only won two from 20 games. That dreadful period in Villa's history was summed up by Pat Murphy of the BBC, when he said it was, "yet another farcical period in Villa's recent history. Garde didn't think much of the players and the feeling was mutual. He was promised players when he signed, but Lerner turned the tap off and he felt badly let down. I don't think Villa could go any lower, but the players who got them into this situation are still standing. They should be looking over their shoulders."

So, who would be next in at Villa Park?

Things weren't going to plan for 20-year-old Jack Grealish, he was going nowhere fast. Not a regular in the Villa side and being on the wrong side of several managers because of his partying, he needed to change things for the sake of his career. He wasn't high profile and he wasn't showing the potential the Villa backroom staff knew he had.

With Rémi Garde's departure, Eric Black took charge for the next game, a home game with Chelsea, and the home fans were restless, given the dire situation on and off the pitch. Even some of the first team players were disconsolate, including Leandro Bacuna, who had spoken of his desire to leave the club. It seemed the discipline had disappeared on the pitch, as well as off it, as nearly half the Villa side got into the book, with Alan Hutton seeing red. Still, Jack was back, on as a 66th minute substitute for Carles Gil, but he made little difference. The 4 – 0 defeat and the final whistle was greeted with resounding boos from the Villa fans, who had suffered a dreadful time. One banner summed up the feeling:

"**No Fight, No Pride, No Effort, No Hope!!**"

After yet another home defeat with Bournemouth, Villa were eventually relegated for the first time since 1987 after a 1 – 0 defeat at Old Trafford on 16th April 2016, with the club 15 points from safety and four games left of the season to complete. It was a sorry day, and Jack didn't even get on the field.

Jack only appeared for a total of 67 minutes during Eric Black's seven games in charge, all as substitute. During those seven games, Villa lost six of them and drew against Newcastle, finishing the season with a record low points' tally of 17, and a – 49 goal difference.

As a boyhood Villa fan himself, Jack felt the impact of relegation more than most of his team- mates after enduring a turbulent 12 months, both personally and professionally, as his side dropped out of the Premier League with barely a whimper and amid unprecedented acrimony and hostility from the Villa fans. Jack had appeared in 16 games that season and unfortunately, Villa lost all of them. It was a dreadful record – and it was the worst season ever! Where would Villa go now, and what was in store for Jack? "It was difficult because we got relegated so early, it was probably one of the worse seasons in the club's history," Jack told AVTV.

"As a Villa fan all my life it was horrible to see," Jack told The Telegraph in 2016. "You're used to seeing the club in the top division and that's what made it worse. I feel like I could have contributed more but the injuries and off-field issues made it difficult." Jack also gave an indication what his relationship with Rémi Garde was actually like, and it came as no surprise to find it out it wasn't the best. "It started well after scoring against Leicester and beating Birmingham in the League Cup but I found it much harder when Rémi Garde came in. It was difficult to get on with him."

I guess those comments came as no surprise to Villa fans.

Suddenly, all the talk was about when Jack would leave Villa, as they faced a battle to keep him during the summer of 2016. Jack spent the early summer at the Toulon Tournament in France and impressed for England Under-21s, but back home it was all kicking off behind the scenes. A host of Premier League clubs were looking at Jack after his excellent performances for Gareth Southgate's Under-21s; Stoke City, Spurs and Everton were said to be sniffing around.

****

Season 2016 – 2017

With the club now in the second tier of English football for the first time in 29 years, the club needed wholesale root and branch reform, from inside to outside, on and off the pitch, starting with the ownership of the club. After putting the club up for sale in May 2014, Randy Lerner finally found what was seen at the time as a reputable buyer for Aston Villa. On 18th May 2016, a sale was agreed to the Recon Group, owned by Chinese businessman Dr Xia Jiantong (AKA Tony Xia). The sale was completed on 14th June 2016 for a reported £76 million after being approved by the Football League.

Dr Xia's first job was to appoint a new manager to hopefully lead the club back into the Premier League and that man was Roberto Di Matteo. Speaking as a Villa fan myself, it was another surprise choice to say the least, although he did have Championship pedigree, having steered West Bromwich Albion to promotion in 2010. He also managed Chelsea to an FA Cup and Champions League double in 2012, so he had some claim to become Aston Villa manager, I guess.

Di Matteo appointed his former Chelsea team-mate, Steve Clarke as first team coach. It seemed like a stroke of genius; Clarke was a well-respected coach in his own right and had the right credentials to be successful as a manager himself. As for the Villa fans, they were split on the appointment of the Italian, some expecting a 'big name' to be put in to replace Garde and the expectation was for the club to be promoted straight away, if not in the second season. A third season in the Championship was unthinkable. However, the Championship has always been an unforgiving league and it doesn't care about reputation or history of a club. It was going to be a long, hard journey for Aston Villa.

Roberto Di Matteo was immediately given money to spend by Dr Xia, and lots of it. Following his arrival, he signed nine players for a combined outlay of around £50m, while 17 players left, worth in the region of £16m between them. Big money was spent on the likes of Jonathan Kodjia (£15m), Ross McCormack (£12m), James Chester (£8m) and others like Richie de Laet, Albert Adomah and Mile Jedinak to name but a few.

It was expected to be a big season for Jack as well. Jack seemed to be favouring a stay at the club, dismissing the host of clubs who were apparently looking for his signature. Expectation grew with the signings, maybe falsely, but the hope was for a good season. "It's a huge season for me and the club. I'm so determined to prove people wrong this season and do it for myself. I want to get this club back where it belongs," Jack told the Telegraph. "I look back on that Liverpool (FA Cup semi-final) game and I'm hoping for more times like that. That was by far the best day of my life. There was no pressure on us and I felt like a little kid going to play on a park that day. This season it's all going to be about hard work."

His summer holiday could not have been more different to any other. Jack disclosed he was focused on his fitness throughout his stay in Dubai and Santorini. He said he was "running on the beaches in the morning. I had a personal trainer with me. I was also going to the gym in the evenings at 7pm when my girlfriend wanted to go out for dinner so I wasn't too popular!"

The relationship with Di Matteo seemed to start nicely according to Jack, "A few days after the new manager was appointed he rang me while I was on my holiday. For him to call me and have a positive chat gave me a really good feeling." But I guess all manager / player relationships start that way, some carry on and last, but some deteriorate.

Even though Di Matteo was said to be a disciplinarian, it looked like nothing had changed for Jack. "We are going to have our rules, our code of conduct and if someone steps outside there are certainly going to be consequences," he was quoted as saying when he took charge of the club. However, two days before an important away game to Barnsley on 27th September, Jack was fined two weeks' wages following off-field indiscretions, which allegedly concerned an all-night party at a Birmingham hotel on the Saturday evening, after the goalless draw at Ipswich.

It was so disappointing, especially given the indication from Jack after the last incident under Remi Garde that he wouldn't get into those situations again. The manager was understood to be annoyed and disappointed at the incident, especially after a series of other incidents involving Villa players. It was obvious that Jack would face the consequences for his actions, "I cannot confirm or deny if he will be available. It's a timing issue and we want to get it right. In general, for the sake of any player they need to learn about what it takes to be an athlete. He needs to grow up very quickly. It's not the first time and he needs to understand if he wants a good career he has to stop." Di Matteo wasn't impressed.

Even the Villa owner, Tony Xia got involved, saying Jack should "avoid going in the wrong direction" following the allegations.

Not only were the club disappointed with Jack at the time, ex-Villa legend, Dion Dublin weighed in by saying, "He is a player that could achieve a lot but I think he's letting himself down, letting the club down, letting the fans down. People around him aren't helping. Get your finger out, do your job, earn your money."

It was time a when Jack needed to buckle down (again) and prove he was the real deal.

A disastrous 3 – 1 League Cup exit away to Luton Town was the blueprint for the season ahead, Villa only winning once in the first 11 League games, with Jack featuring in 9, scoring two goals. The team couldn't turn draws into wins and it cost them dearly in their league position of 19th; those 11 games only returned one win and seven draws. The season was turning into a disaster. Their problem was conceding late goals, which could have been put down to lack of concentration at the back. The form was not good enough to get promoted or reach the play-offs, let alone stay in the league. To top it all, the team were booed off by their fans after the 2 - 0 defeat at Preston on 1st October. It is said that once you lose the support of the travelling fans and they turn on you, you're in trouble, and it was true after that game. The board were becoming increasingly frustrated after envisaging at the start of the season, Villa should be around the play-off positions by that stage and Di Matteo was quickly relieved of his position after that embarrassing defeat

It was yet another frustrating time for Jack, for Villa, and for their fans, with the manager merry-go-round set to continue. Since 2010, 12 managers or caretaker managers had come and gone, with five managers in the previous 18 months including the sacking of Di Matteo. Assistant Head Coach, Steve Clarke, moved up to take charge for the short term. Clarke had managerial experience having spent a year and a half in charge at West Bromwich Albion, so the team was in good hands, even though it would be briefly.

Not surprisingly, Clarke's reign didn't last long, in fact he didn't even take charge of a game as there was an international break. The board acted quickly and appointed Steve Bruce as their new manager, the favourite with the Bookies, but not with the fans, who immediately related him with their local rivals, Birmingham City, even though that was 10 years previously - some fans never forget things like that, and the appointment wound up the locals. Having said that, no one could dispute his Championship managerial record, having taken Birmingham (twice) and Hull (twice) up into the Premier League and that was the mantra for picking Bruce – to get the club promoted in the first season, if not the second.

As soon as Steve Bruce arrived, he appointed Colin Calderwood as his assistant and Stephen Clemence as his first-team coach.

Bruce's first task was to improve on early-season results, which was easier said than done. The first game in charge was a local derby with Wolves at Villa Park which ended in another draw, followed by an away trip to Reading. Villa hadn't won an away league game for 18 months, but a late Jordan Ayew penalty gave them a well-deserved victory to settle the nerves of the fans, and maybe change their impression of the manager. Bruce even praised the 5,000 travelling fans, "I have to pay special mention to the supporters in the last 10 minutes. They breathed life into the lads. For a club that's been in trouble, over the past couple of years in particular, to have 5,000 fans at Reading on a Tuesday night is remarkable." He also took a swipe at Roberto Di Matteo by saying, "The previous management lost 10 points from goals conceded in the last few minutes of games. If they hadn't, I probably wouldn't be here."

Bruce's start at the helm of rudderless Villa took them on a seven-game unbeaten run, winning four and drawing three, something that was virtually unheard of for the previous four or five seasons. The brilliant early form briefly diminished Bruce's association with Birmingham City amongst the fanbase and everything was a bit rosier at Villa Park at that point in time. Jack missed a few games during that initial spell but returned for the 2 – 1 win against Blackburn on Bonfire Night.

Their form continued to be steady up until the turn of the year when Villa lost eight out of nine games and that's when the alarm bells started to ring aloud for Villa fans. Jack saw red in an away game in early February with a second yellow card, before watching his team lose to a late winner scored by 17-year-old Ben Brereton who fired in from Assombalonga's header to win it for Nottingham Forest. That defeat left Villa in 14th after 29 games, 13 points behind the play-off places.

The Championship is an unforgiving league and there was going to be no special treatment for Aston Villa.

However, that poor form from 2nd January until 20th February was reversed as the team won seven from eight games to silence the critics and finished the season strongly, eventually finishing 13th in the Championship with 62 points, which wasn't great, but better than expected if you look back at their position back in early October. Jack appeared in 33 games in the Championship, but still wasn't considered an automatic choice in the midfield, starting some games from the bench, scoring five goals, the second-highest scorer behind Jonathan Kodjia, who repaid some of his big transfer fee, scoring 19 goals.

Season 2017 - 2018

The summer of 2017 was to be another rebuilding job at Villa Park, and the major signing was bringing in former Chelsea captain, John Terry (JT) who was immediately made club captain. It was a masterstroke by Bruce, who managed to persuade JT to come to Villa while on the golf course. There wasn't much other business done during the summer transfer window, with Ahmed Elmohamady and Glen Whelan brought in as experienced players to bolster the defence, but there weren't any eye-opening signings. There were some other deals done, but they were the loan signings of Axel Tuanzebe and Robert Snodgrass.

As for Jack, it was again meant to be a big season for him, but the pre-season ended in disaster. The 21-year-old suffered a freak injury during Villa's final pre-season game on 29th July 2017 against Watford at Villa Park, which ended goalless. A seemingly innocuous collision with Watford midfielder and former teammate, Tom Cleverley left Jack on the ground in pain holding his ribs. It didn't look good for him, as the fans looked on in anguish - Jack was stretchered off and it later emerged that the impact had caused a bleed in one of his kidneys.

Speaking to AVTV, he recalled the moment he picked up the injury, "The ball bounced on the edge of the box and I thought to myself 'I have to get this, I can't let the gaffer down'. I went up for the header and then obviously I've got caught by Clevs (Tom Cleverley). Obviously he didn't mean it – we are close friends. When it first happened, I didn't think about the pain at all, I just thought 'the ball has gone, I'm going to be in trouble here'."

Jack suggested the after-effects of the collision was ten-times worse than being winded by Cleverley and when he got to his feet, he couldn't think about walking, let alone running again in that game. He said it felt like he'd been shot and started shouting in pain to the medics.

The extent of his injury wasn't known at the time, but news of the injury emerged when Jack posted on his social media accounts:
"Absolutely devastated. Got a nasty elbow to the stomach in yesterday's game which caused a bleed in my kidney. Had a mini op early this morning and will now be out for at least 2 - 3 months. Gutted as season was about to start next week but will be doing everything to come back fitter and stronger. Up the Villa."

He subsequently told the Daily Mirror, "I took a kick to the kidney and it split in two places. It was pouring with blood, internally, for about five hours. It's the worst pain I've ever been in. I went to Heartlands Hospital in Birmingham. They found out what it was and I was rushed to the Queen Elizabeth (Hospital) for an operation. Before it happened, the surgeon had to tell me the consequences of what could happen if it didn't work. He looked me in the eye and said, 'Jack, you could die'. My reply was, 'What?' I was genuinely scared. I was expecting to be back inside a week, but it was three or four months. I knew Tom Cleverley from our time together at Villa and he couldn't believe it. I spoke to him the morning after the operation and I said, 'Mate, do you know where I am and what's happened?' He couldn't have been more apologetic."

Jack seemed very philosophical of the news of the injury and its prognosis, "I'm a big believer that everything happens for a reason. I came back from that injury a different person. I thought about how everything could be taken away from you in such a short space of time. I worked so hard to come back because I missed football. I wanted to be the best I could be. I was in the gym every day and my energy is so much better. I feel stronger, fitter."

In hindsight, those words could be attributed to the new-found strength and determination to succeed that Jack subsequently found - it also resulted in a more mature Jack Grealish, but more about that later.

It was a bitter blow to the season for Villa and for Jack, who only had made 44 starts in over three seasons playing for the first team due to a series of injuries and suspensions - and a succession of managers not picking him.

The disappointing news concerning Jack came as the new skipper, John Terry suggested that only winning the title will do for Aston Villa, "Nothing else is really acceptable for me as an individual and how I have behaved and what I have been around in previous years."

The season started in the similar vein as the previous five or six, mostly with defeat and draws, until a 3 – 0 away win at Barnsley on 16th September sprung them into life at last.

The prognosis of Jack's injury suggested he would be out for a period of around three months and it wasn't until the 4th November 2017 at the home game against Sheffield Wednesday that he was fit enough to make the bench and to make his first appearance of the season; however, he couldn't prevent his team suffering their fourth defeat of the season.

It wasn't until the away defeat at Derby on 16th December that Jack made his first start of the season following the kidney operation in late July, even though he'd made several substitute appearances before the Derby defeat. At that point Villa were still in the play-off places after 22 games.

Jack's influence on games had become noticeable by that time and his stamina, stature and fitness had become remarkably more pronounced than it ever had been before. Jack had been a marked man for the two seasons in the Championship but it seemed he was running more and influencing games right up until the final minutes. Kicking Jack Grealish was not a new tactic; in fact, even his academy pal sometimes resorted to fouling him as a means to stop him in his tracks.

So, what or who had influenced that change in Jack's game?

That new-found fitness wasn't just down to Jack's desire to get back playing for Villa, it was more down to an old academy pal called Oli Stevenson.

Little was known about Oli Stevenson. He joined Villa as an eight-year-old but wasn't as lucky as Jack as he was released early on and never made it as a player. However, he later decided to embark on a new career as a coach (at Villa) and decided to go and study Sports Science at Loughborough University with the support of the club. It was the lifeline he wanted and he really made the most of it. Oli then progressed from teaching the young kids and stepped up to be a fitness coach with the first-team. His workouts were said to be strenuous but engaging and he even earned the respect of the then Villa captain, John Terry and other senior pros, including Jack. He was always pushing himself to do well, and his application to go one step further had obviously worked well with Jack when he came back from his kidney injury because it was obvious the results were showing on the pitch.

It was also noticeable that Jack's upper body had changed; he wasn't the most muscular player on the park, but it was obvious looking at him after his long absence that he had been working on that. Again, Oli Stevenson was credited to the improvements in Jack's appearance that made him more powerful. Former Villa player, Lewis Kinsella told the Birmingham Mail, "He's always had big leg muscles, calves and quads, but when he was younger his upper body strength wasn't that good. Oli has been working with him and he looks more powerful and is driving with the ball. The stamina comes with experience because he is learning how and when to use his energy. It will also be the regular football; this must be one of the longest runs he's had in the first team."

Come early February, Villa were riding high in the Championship and by the time they beat local rivals, Birmingham City 2 – 0 on 11th February, they were 2nd and recorded their seventh straight victory (for the first time since February 1990) with Jack playing. This was probably his best game for the first-team up until that point. He was starting to show the kind of form that took the eye of the national media a couple of seasons previously, and he took the man-of-the-match award for his performance, which included an assist for Albert Adomah's opening goal in the 60th minute. Villa fans knew how hard he had worked to get back to full fitness since his kidney operation and the extra effort was starting to pay dividends, just in time for the end of season run in for the promotion and play-off places.

When Villa played fellow promotion rivals Cardiff City on 10th April, one place separated the two sides but Jack's spectacular second-half volley from 20 yards secured the points for the Villans in front of the TV cameras and was watched in the stands by Villa fan, Prince William, who was accompanied by former Villa striker, John Carew. In a feisty encounter, it took a bit of magic from Jack to break the deadlock with five minutes to spare. It was only Jack's third goal of the season but it was probably his most important goal of his career to date, and probably his best.

Villa were stuck at 4th place in the league for the remainder of the season so qualified for the play-offs, where they met Middlesbrough in the semi-final (4th played 6th). Jack was in the action again in the first-leg at The Riverside, when his corner kick reached the head of Mile Jedinak who fired the ball into the net. It was enough to give the visitors a 1 – 0 first-leg lead to take back to Villa Park. Manager Steve Bruce said of Jack, "Jack is starting to mature, he's looking up to people like John Terry and Glenn Whelan who do it properly." He was certainly on fire and desperate to get his side back into the Premier League.

The second-leg ended in a drab scoreless draw but it was enough to send Villa into the EFL Championship Play-Off Final to face Fulham, who disposed of Cardiff City over two legs.

Even though Jack hadn't played the whole season, he had grown considerably as a player and he attributed the newfound maturity and improved decision making in his game to both the coaching staff and influence of senior members of the squad, including captain John Terry. As a fan watching him closely, you could see he had started to control the midfield and he didn't flit in and out of games like he used to in his early days when he was inconsistent. He had begun to dictate the tempo for the Villa side with mazy hip-shaking swerves through midfield or his expansive, progressive passing from deep.

In a team full of veterans and experience, he had quietly become the player his teammates first looked to, and that is testament to the player he had become. Speaking after the play-off semi-final, Jack said, "This time last year the manager would have brought me off. In the last three months, 95 per cent of the time I've played 90 minutes. The manager believes in me, the coaching staff believe in me and the likes of JT have helped me on and off the pitch. It's given me the confidence to go and play."

Jack was mobbed by fans for his performance after Villa's second-leg draw against Middlesbrough. He had hopes of repaying the faith the manager had shown in him, who also had a difficult time after sadly losing both his parents within the space of a few months.

Jack spoke of that faith Steve Bruce had shown in him when he was in hospital with the kidney trouble at the start of the season, "When I was in hospital, he came to see me twice and he Facetimed me every other day to see how I was. You remember stuff like that and if I do end up scoring the winner, I'll dedicate it to him."

So, Villa and Fulham were Wembley bound for the EFL Championship Play-Off Final on 26th May 2018. The date is synonymous with the club winning the European Cup in 1982, so Villa fans were feeling reminiscent about the prospect of another famous victory for their team. The Londoners were undoubted favourites to win the one-off game, the richest domestic football game in the world, worth an estimated £170m to the winner. Villa were in desperate need to win because failure meant that they would be heavily restricted by the devil that is Financial Fair Play (FFP).

It turned out to be a fractious game and of course, Jack was involved in everything. Fulham captain, Tom Cairney scored, what turned out to be the only goal of the game on 23 minutes. The game exploded into action later in the first-half when Ryan Fredricks was sent-off for showing his studs to Jack. In the second-half, Jack fell in the penalty area under a challenge by Matt Targett (now a Villa player) but nothing was given by the referee. Villa looked the more likely to score the next goal, but then, in the 70th minute, Fulham centre-back, Denis Odoi was sent-off for two bookable offences, both committed on Jack. The red-card poured pressure on Fulham but Villa couldn't find a way past the Fulham back-line and the Londoners held on to clinch the win and were promoted.

It wasn't a spectacle but Fulham fans didn't care about that, their club were in the Premier League. For Villa and for Jack, they were left with ifs and buts; what if Jack hadn't have been injured for the first three months of the season; what if Jonathan Kodjia hadn't of picked up an injury which left him out for most of the campaign; what if Ryan Fredricks had of been sent-off.

On the day, Villa just weren't good enough, but Jack was their stand-out performer at Wembley - he was outstanding, almost scored one of the best goals ever in a Play-Off Final and didn't deserve to be on the losing side, but that's football, I guess.

One major positive that had come out of the season was his consistent form during the second half of the campaign and the club were under no illusion that it was going to be hard for them to keep hold of their star player during the summer; keeping the 22-year-old at Villa Park was the major task facing the club and was paramount to Steve Bruce's side mounting another challenge for promotion in the 2018 – 2019 campaign.

Villa spent heavily during the first two seasons in the Championship in their bid to return to the top-flight but defeat at Wembley was going to cost them dearly.

The cloth was going to be cut accordingly (again) as they prepared for a third successive season in the second tier; it was the "unthinkable" scenario, but it was reality.

Chapter 5

WILL HE STAY, OR WILL HE GO?

After the Wembley defeat, Jack attracted the attention of the Premier League 'big boys'.

"The discussions have got to be had above me to say what we've got and what we haven't got," Steve Bruce said just after the EFL Championship Play-Off Final defeat to Fulham on 26th May 2018. He added that it is up to veteran captain John Terry to decide whether he will play on at Villa Park next season. Bruce also made it clear that he was under no illusion about Jack's future, and it would probably end up being out of his control, "Of course there will be speculation about Jack. Personally, I would like him to stay. Another year with us would do him the world of good. We'd love to have given him the platform of the Premier League and we haven't, but he's playing regular football week in and week out. We'll see what happens."

It had become well-documented during the 2017 – 2018 season that Jack Grealish longed to play in the Premier League again - and preferably for Aston Villa. As soon as the final whistle blew at Wembley the odds-on Jack Grealish leaving his boyhood club grew by the day. There were problems developing behind the scenes, financial problems that had dire consequences for the club, all on the back of that 1 – 0 defeat to Fulham. Villa owner Tony Xia had bankrolled the club, threw the dice and lost. It was as simple as that; he had banked on basically winning one game, and that was the EFL Championship Play-Off Final.

When the dust had settled on the Wembley disaster, it was becoming clear what a mess the football club was actually in. Multiple loans had been taken out just to pay the monthly bills, which were mounting up by the day. James Chester and Jack Grealish, arguably Villa's two most valuable players, were all set to be sold to Stoke City and Tottenham Hotspur, respectively.

On 5th June 2018, Villa missed the deadline to pay a £4 million tax bill, and the club was faced with a winding up order and the real possibility of going out of business. A day later, Tony Xia suspended and later dismissed CEO Keith Wyness, after he was alleged to have discussed the prospect of Aston Villa's possible administration and subsequent 12-point deduction with third parties without Xia's knowledge. It was very serious indeed. Then, on the very next day, 7th June 2018, Xia managed to negotiate an agreement with HMRC to pay £500,000 of the £4 million bill, promising to pay the remaining portion at a later date. That saved the club from immediate danger, but Xia confirmed that the club was still in significant financial difficulty.

What did that mean for Steve Bruce and the team? Well, for a start, Steve Bruce was kept on as manager, mainly because the club couldn't afford to pay him out of his huge contract. Secondly, it had to cut back on the wages and sell off some of the main assets, even though, with the exception of Jack Grealish himself, the playing staff wasn't worth a fortune. Out went the likes of John Terry, Carles Gil, Jordan Amavi and Pierluigi Gollini and in came a host of loan players, including Axel Tuanzebe, Tyrone Mings, Yannick Bolasie, Anwar El Ghazi and Tammy Abraham. Surprisingly, all the loans players were very good players, young and hungry, so on that front it looked good. With the exception of an ageing JT, the other players who were let go were no great loss. On a positive note, Villa legend, Alan Hutton signed an improved one-year deal.

The 2018 – 2019 season was most definitely a boom or bust scenario; it had to be promotion, or the club would go under. A fourth season in the Championship not worth thinking about.

What did that mean for Jack Grealish?

Jack had become 'a serious footballer' and of course, Villa didn't want to sell, but it was obvious they needed to sell some of their 'silverware' just to survive. Jack increasingly became their pawn during the summer, as they had to raise upwards of £40 million if they were to comply with Financial Fair Play regulations. After heavy spending led to an unsuccessful bid for promotion back to the Premier League last season, Steve Bruce was quoted as saying, "Jack will have to be sold."

The attacking midfielder enjoyed a very productive 2017–2018 season and took the eye to several clubs outside of the Championship. If the club had sold him the revenue gained would have undoubtedly helped to alleviate the club's financial troubles – in the short-term anyway. After being loosely linked with the likes of Manchester United, Newcastle United and Leicester City, Tottenham were publicly making more serious moves for Jack, and their manager, Mauricio Pochettino made no bones about wanting him in his squad for the up-coming season at White Hart Lane. Spurs were reportedly interested in securing a cut-price deal for Jack, with some suggesting they had hoped to agree a deal worth £20m. That sort of money wouldn't have bought a player of Jack's quality back in 2014, let alone in 2018. The Spurs manager apparently wanted to groom Jack in the way he had done with Dele Alli. However, any move for Jack would have been seen as taking advantage of the money problems Villa had at the time. Spurs were adamant Villa were going to cash in on their prized asset as Villa were not in a good bargaining stance, but it was crucial to stick to their guns and not let Jack go on the cheap. Daniel Levy, not one for wanting to spend over the odds, initially believed he could tempt Villa with a menial £15m, which was a joke really; Levy must have been on another planet if he thought he could have got away with that.

Villa's financial vulnerability had fuelled speculation that Jack was about to depart his boyhood club all summer. Rumours circulated the media that Tottenham were about to take advantage of Villa's darkest moment with a derisory offer of £3m cash, with Josh Onomah coming the other way as a makeweight. No disrespect to Josh Onomah, but that very suggestion was outrageous! Whether that was true or not, we may never know, but Spurs' UEFA Cup winning captain, Graham Roberts spoke out in the media to quell any speculation, saying the deal was "not true".

Although Villa were in need for funds, they were never that desperate! Villa knew the game Spurs were playing and that wasn't going to happen.

Although no value had been put on Jack's head by the Villa board, they obviously had a figure in mind that they would negotiate with (if and when that time came) and £20m was well below that figure. Steve Bruce told Sky News, "There will be nobody feeling sorry for Aston Villa because financially we have got ourselves in a bit of a pickle, so yes we have got to be ready for that. I have enjoyed working with Jack, and he is the obvious one that clubs are going to target because he had a wonderful six months. He reminded everybody as a 22-year-old what a very good player he is. On another day at Wembley, he could have scored one of the great Wembley goals. He is a special talent, a real special talent, and yes, you don't want to lose him but the inevitable thing is we have to. We have to in order to keep the club up and running and keep it in line with Financial Fair Play." Bruce also said, "There are going to be people that I do not want to sell - and the obvious one is Jack - but people will know that we have got financial problems and they'll sit and wait, and wait, till deadline day possibly. I hope that doesn't happen but we've got to batten down the hatches and wait for it."

Behind the scenes, it subsequently transpired that Tony Xia had been putting the feelers out for fresh investment even before the defeat at Wembley. However, not even the most die-hard Villa fan would have expected, or even dreamt of, what actually materialised during late July and the start of the 2018 – 2019 season.

Somehow, Dr Xia had pulled off a miracle and found the club's saviours and just in time.

It emerged on 20th July 2018 that an Egyptian company called the NSWE group, which was owned by the Egyptian billionaire Nassef Sawiris and the American billionaire Wes Edens were to invest in the football club. They had purchased a controlling 55% stake in the club at a cost of a reported £30m and Sawiris took over the role of executive chairman, with Edens taking the role of co-chairman. However, Xia initially remained as another co-chairman. Apparently, the whole deal took nine days to thrash out.

What the Villa fans were most interested in was the wealth of the two new owners. Sawiris was said to have a personal wealth of around £5.2bn, making him the richest Egyptian in the world and Edens, co-owner of the Milwaukee Bucks, a National Basketball Association (NBA) franchise based in Milwaukee, Wisconsin, was estimated to be worth around £1.9bn. Their combined wealth immediately made them the third richest owners in English football.

Christmas had come early to Aston Villa Football Club.

When the deal was made public the owners issued a joint statement which said:

"As lifelong football fans, we are excited and privileged to have become part of this great club. We believe that together we bring business and sports experience that will help strengthen the club to ensure Aston Villa can return to its rightful place in the upper echelons of English football."

"Our goal is to bring sustainable success to the club, building on its rich history while respecting its loyal fan base and unique culture. We understand that we are stewards of Aston Villa on behalf of the fans and we take that responsibility seriously."

"We look forward to working with Dr Tony to undertake a thorough assessment and evaluation of the club in the coming weeks and our priority is to strengthen the squads and structures ahead of the upcoming season and beyond."

Villa fans were always very sceptical of the assumed wealth of Dr Tony Xia, who in the end, couldn't get the money out of China to feed the club. The money ran dry and the bills didn't get paid. He became as unpopular as Randy Lerner ended up before him, but all of a sudden, from almost bankruptcy one minute to becoming extremely rich the next, Aston Villa's financial future had been sorted in the space of nine days.

While all that was going on, behind the scenes the future of Jack

Grealish was still lingering on and Pochettino was still determined to sign him, even though the clubs' financial future looked a little different. Suddenly, Villa's bargaining stance had improved and any club wanting to buy Jack would have to stump up an extortionate amount of money. However, no club had made an official bid for him and given Villa's newfound wealth, there was no reliance on selling their prized asset anymore.

How things can change in football in such a short space of time. One minute Villa fans were despondent because of the disappointment of Wembley, the impending financial crisis and the imminent departure of 'Super Jack', the next they were in seventh heaven and feeling like they'd won the European Cup again.

The closer it got to the start of the season, the less likely it seemed that Jack was going to be sold, but the club were conscious that football is a cruel game and clubs would be waiting until the last day of the transfer window to try their hand and get Jack, and others, on the cheap. However, with their newfound monetary strength, Steve Bruce had made it clear that Jack was no longer for sale at any cost, "There've been discussions and that's been going on practically all summer. The one thing the (new) owners have made pretty clear is that no one is for sale. We don't want to lose our best players. They're aware, though, that every player has got his price. The good thing the owners have been able to do is not let anybody go on the cheap. If anybody wants to come and buy our players, they're going to have to find a premium and make sure the owners are comfortable with it."

The new season, which was looking to be one of doom and gloom for the Villa fans, had been turned on its head, thanks to Sawiris and Edens. The fans were looking forward to the season with anticipation, rather than dread. More importantly, the long-term future of the club was again looking as bright as it's past once was.

However, while Villa may had been made seemingly 'cash-rich' almost overnight, they still needed to meet the Football Fair Play (FFP) guidelines considering the significant losses made over the past few seasons in the Championship. That would carry on throughout the season, despite the owners pumping money into the club to make it stable.

Season 2018 - 2019

The opening game of the season was an away trip to Steve Bruce's former club, Hull City on 6th August. Jack was in the side to face Hull but even at that late stage, his future was uncertain. With the transfer window about to shut, no club had come in for Jack; no one had made an official bid and as it transpired, all the talk was in the media, but while there was talk, his future made the headlines.

Villa seemed to have put their troubled summer behind them as they came from behind to win the game at Hull, quite easily in fact. However, the away fans were left stunned in the 83rd minute when Jack was surprisingly substituted, replaced by Bjarnason. As Jack waved at the fans and left the field to rapturous reception from the thousands of travelling Villa fans, it seemed a bit like a farewell reception, given the transfer window was about to shut in a matter of days.

Did he know something every other Villa fan didn't?

As it transpired, the waving and emotional events of that balmy August night in Hull were all in vain as the transfer window shut firmly for another summer and Jack Grealish was still an Aston Villa player; no club had made an offer for the midfield talisman. That chapter in the short career of Jack Grealish had been closed, for another season anyway. According to sources close to Jack, he was convinced at once stage he was leaving his boyhood club during the close-season, and even just three days before the end of the transfer window on 9th August his future was in doubt. The prospect of playing in the Premier League, as well as the Champions League for Spurs was tempting for him but the arrival of Sawiris and Edens was the gamechanger that Jack was probably wishing for (well, maybe wishful thinking) and immediately changed the cards on the table.

After the 3 - 1 opening day win at Hull, I remember thinking it looked like an emotional farewell. Jack subsequently spoke to talkSPORT and explained why he waved to the fans, "It was close. At Hull, I was 95 per-cent sure it was going to be my last game. I waved to the fans when I got taken off as I thought I was going. Even on the Thursday morning of the transfer window, I thought I was leaving. Before the new owners [arrived], Villa needed the money so I kind of accepted that me going would save the club. I think the fans would have taken that, too, because we needed the money. Of course, it was unsettling, it was all summer. A lot of people saw the interview with the manager in Portugal when he said the club would have to sell me. At that time, it could have got done, but for whatever reason it didn't. They [Spurs] weren't willing to pay what Villa wanted at the time. But the new owners came in and they changed everything."

Conjecture over Jack's Villa future was finally ended once and for all, when new owner Nassef Sawiris told Tottenham and Daniel Levy via the media, "we don't need your money."

For Jack, he had only one ambition for the season ahead, "Getting promotion with Villa is still the ultimate for me. It's what I've always dreamed of and playing there in the Premier League is still the big aim."

Normal service had resumed.

Three weeks after the transfer window had closed on 9th August, Villa headhunted Christian Purslow as their CEO. He had vast experience in football, having been MD at Liverpool and Head of Global Activities at Chelsea. It was an astute appointment by the owners, an important and a well-timed appointment, too. However, it was the going to become the biggest job on his CV and probably the hardest.

It was by no coincidence that Purslow's first job was to get Jack signed up and his immediate future secured. During the first week in September, Jack finally agreed and signed a new five-year contract worth a reported £35,000-a-week and it was a major coup for Purslow. The complete contrast between June and August was staggering and it convinced Jack that his immediate future was at Villa and he was determined to get his club back into the Premier League, where they belonged.

When the ink had dried on the mega deal and the season had got well under way, Jack spoke to The Telegraph of "disappointment" of the collapsed move to Spurs, and an insight to where his mind was during the summer, "You've got to look at what Spurs have done this season. They've beaten Manchester United 3 – 0 at Old Trafford, they're playing Barcelona in the Champions League next week. I felt that if I'd gone there I could have maybe been in the England squad by the end of the year. I would never have gone there just to make up the numbers. I would have been a squad player, obviously, because you have to look at how good their players are. But I genuinely thought that after a month or two of training, I could have really made an impact. At the start of the season my head was swivelled, it was all over the place. Even after the transfer window closed, until the end of August, I wasn't right."

Jack subsequently spoke to talkSPORT about the unsettling summer and was philosophical about the situation, "I truly think that everything happens for a reason." However, the part of that interview Villa fans will be pleased about was when Jack said, "It's not like I was devastated it didn't happen, though, because I've still got to realise how lucky I am to be playing for my boyhood club. I've played over 100 games for Villa and I've only just turned 23."

No doubt, leaving Villa would have been a tremendous wrench for Jack; anyone who has followed his career can see just how much he loves Aston Villa and how much playing for them means to him. Which is something special coming from a professional footballer these days, and that's why the fans adore him so much. I would imagine his father, Kevin and his family were tremendously supportive of him during that summer, just as they have been throughout his career – and I guess they were a little pleased he didn't sign for the North London club.

Suddenly, Aston Villa Football Club were in good hands, and managed to keep hold of both of their prized assets (Grealish and Chester). It was now time to put the uncertainty to an end and to get through another 46 games of the Championship season - and hopefully more.

****

Villa were struggling at the start of the season, with two defeats in 11 in the League but were drawing too many games (six) and were mid-table. Things weren't really going to plan yet again. Steve Bruce was under some pressure, not only from the new board, but from the fans. The ex-Birmingham City boss was being reminded about his past by the fans once again and before the home game against Preston a fan threw a cabbage at Bruce and he was subjected to abuse from some sections of the crowd who were calling for him to be sacked. Bruce was philosophical about it all, "it's up to others to decide what happens now." Only a 97th minute equaliser from veteran Glenn Whelan saved his blushes, after the home side surrendered a two-goal lead in that Preston game. As for the cabbage incident, Bruce was angry, "The guy is being questioned...unfortunately, it sums up the society we are in at the moment. There's no respect for anyone. I find the whole thing hugely disrespectful."

The very next day, Steve Bruce was relieved of his position. The board had either listened to the fans or had made a big judgement call.

It was well documented that Jack had a good relationship with Steve Bruce and great respect for him; Bruce had supported him throughout the time he was out with his kidney injury. Now he had to start again with yet another manager.

That man was Dean Smith.

Smith was the manager of Brentford and was respected for building teams who play an attractive passing game, something that Villa fans have not seen for a long while; Steve Bruce's style of football was always criticised by fans as lacking tactics and boring. Smith's appointment was seen as a complete change in direction for Villa and his job was to reinvigorate the team – and the fans. Smith was also a Villa fan, and his appointment was greeted by the faithful with absolute joy. They really couldn't believe their luck of late, even though the club were well off the mark in the League. What's more, Villa favourite, John Terry was appointed as Smith's assistant coach, coming back in after a few months out of the game following his retirement from playing.

Youth team coach, Kevin MacDonald took temporary charge of the away defeat to Millwall and he immediately criticised the players, saying, "I think there are lots of things the new manager will need to address. All the players, individually, need to tidy themselves up. The team as a group need to tidy themselves up. There are individual mistakes from a different player each game. I'm sure it will get tidied up very quickly. If it does, this team will go up the table very quickly."

Smith's 'coming home' party started on 20th October 2018 with a 1 – 0 win against Swansea City in front of a near capacity crowd of 41,326 at Villa Park. It was only their second clean sheet of the season but it was a well-earned victory. That attendance was one of the biggest crowds of the day, including the Premier League. The fans' appetite for football had just intensified with the recruitment of a modern, forward thinking football manager and was 'one of our own'. "It just shows what can happen at our club if we have a plan to move forward," said Smith.

Dean Smith had the fans on side within 90 minutes of football at Villa Park; Steve Bruce had never been on side with most of the fans in the two years he was Villa manager. That opening victory made him the first new Villa manager (of six) to win their first League game since 8th September 2010 and Gérard Houllier.

It was obvious that the appointment of Dean Smith was a marriage made in heaven. For the long-suffering Villa fans who had experienced multiple poor appointments since Martin O'Neill had left the club in August 2010, on the eve of the new season. The former Brentford manager said at the time he could make Jack a better player and stated that he wasn't using the most of his ability and needed to play better without the ball, not just with the ball. During the first week of Smith being in charge, he made Jack run round the Bodymoor Heath training ground without a ball in sight. Smith told the Telegraph, "Jack is an outstanding talent and he was probably rubbing his hands when he saw me coming, thinking this is a guy who wants his teams to play. And then all the work this week has been without the ball. He has probably seen a different side to me but that is part of his game he needs to do a little bit better. He has not got the goals and assists that somebody of his talent should." It was certainly a different approach but anyone following Jack's career could see what he meant. "I invite the players to ask questions and Jack has been asking questions. He has got that desire to get better and I liked the way he was trying to get in the box more."

Jack's first Championship goal of the season came in the home game against Bolton on 2nd November, as he scored the opener within four minutes and made an assist for James Chester with the second on 57 minutes. Smith described Jack's new role, "Jack Grealish did just what was asked of him in getting in the box and scoring. And James Chester put in a really good performance. Quite apart from his goal, that goal-line clearance he pulled off was like another goal." It was their fifth win of the season, not good enough for a team aiming, or rather banking on getting back to the Premier League.

However, it could be said that Jack's performances weren't up to his usual standard. With all of the talk about whether Jack was going to Spurs or staying at Villa during the summer, it took him some time to settle down and get his head right. Jack revealed where his head was to talkSPORT, "For about two months until Steve Bruce got sacked and Dean Smith came in, I was crap; I was nowhere near the way I should have been playing. I think I got one assist, maybe until the start of November, even though I played most games. That's nowhere near good enough, especially for myself and what I expect of myself."

What followed a mixed start to Smith's reign as manager, with two wins and two defeats was a run of good results leading up to the pre-Christmas game with Championship favourites and leaders, Leeds United. A run of four wins and three draws and plenty of goals changed the face of the league, with Villa up to 8th and three points behind Middlesbrough in the play-off places. During that run, Jack scored for the second consecutive home game in the 4 – 2 win against local rivals Birmingham City in front of a full-house. Villa were behind after half-an-hour but two goals in two minutes from Jonathan Kodjia and Jack turned the game to Villa's advantage. Jack's goal, his first against the local rivals was from a diving header from Albert Adomah's wickedly dipping left-foot delivery from the flank, "I don't think I've ever scored with a header in my life, but Albert Adomah put a great ball in at the back stick and I couldn't really miss," he told the Daily Express.

The next home game against Nottingham Forest will be remembered for a very long time. The 32,868 inside Villa Park witnessed what can only be described as "breath-taking" or maybe it was "mayhem". The game had everything, including 10 goals, six bookings, a sending off, and an injury time Tammy Abraham 'winner' disallowed which would have been his fifth goal of the game. Jack was involved as always, as he delivered Abraham's fourth goal from a free-kick to level the scores at 4 – 4. "These kinds of games are great to watch at home on the sofa because it's really entertaining," Tammy Abraham told BBC Radio WM, "But when you're on the pitch it's just end to end and you have to keep getting ready for a chance." Villa boss Smith pointed out that his side had 26 attempts on goal compared to eight for the visitors, adding that keeper Orjan Nyland was not at his busiest, "I don't think our goalkeeper's made a save. said. We're devastated by the fifth goal because that's something we should've been better at."

The game ended 5 – 5, but it could have been anything really, and it meant Villa had scored 16 goals and had taken 13 points from the first seven games of Smith's managerial reign. Not only that, the style of football had also totally changed. Gone was the "keep it tight" football served up from Steve Bruce, replaced by free-flowing attacking football. Games like that Nottingham Forest one don't come round very often, which is all well and good, considering Villa conceded five goals from virtually five shots on target.

Jack played one more game, an away victory at the Riverside before he limped off in the 87th minute of the local derby at The Hawthorns. He looked in pain but nobody, apart from the club medical people, knew what was behind the injury or how bad it was - we wouldn't find out for a while, either. Glenn Whelan replaced Jack, with his side 2 – 1 up. The word "controversial" can be added to the vocabulary when West Bromwich Albion snatched a dramatic draw as the ball clearly struck Jay Rodriguez's arm, not once but twice as he levelled deep into stoppage time. Smith told the Birmingham Mail, "I thought Rodriguez should have been booked for the cynical trip on him (Jack) but I didn't see anyone cautioned. He's been kicked from pillar to post, and for some teams it's finally worked because he's now injured."

Jack's injury was confirmed after a scan showed he had a shin injury. The injury initially left the medical people scratching their heads and no timescales were put on Jack's return, although the early indications showed he would be back for the busy Christmas fixtures. As a precaution, Jack started to wear a protective boot as the medics weren't sure whether it was a bone stress injury or a muscle injury. It came as no real surprise that Jack would be injured badly at some stage of his career. He had become a marked man in the Championship and the most fouled player for the previous two seasons. "All those kicks take their toll on a young player like him, it's not fair on the kid," Smith told the Express & Star.

Whatever the prognosis was, his injury had come at a most inopportune time of the season and the other midfielders would need to step-up to the mark. However, just before the next game, at home to Stoke, Smith confirmed the worse, that he would miss at least three months with a shin injury; Villa would have to do without their talisman for a third of the season if they were to stand any chance of being promoted. It was a bitter blow for Jack and for Villa.

More worryingly, it was subsequently revealed that the injury had been picked up in Dean Smith's first game in charge, at home to Swansea on 20th October, which meant Jack had been playing through the pain barrier for several weeks.

The pressure was on Dean Smith.

During the three-month lay-off, Jack missed a total of 13 League games and the embarrassing FA Cup home defeat to Swansea. To say the form was patchy is an understatement; seven draws, four defeats and only two wins up to Jack's scheduled comeback on 2nd March and a home game to Derby. Villa had struggled for form and found themselves slipping to 11th place, eight points off the play-off places following a run of one win in 10 league outings with 11 games of the season to go. At half-time in the Stoke game, it looked all doom and gloom, with Villa trailing by a single goal, but Dean Smith laid into the players and they came out for the second half, all guns' blazing. An Albert Adomah strike on 62 minutes levelled the score.

Only a miracle could save Villa's season. They desperately needed Jack, to return, but at what cost? They needed him back, not only for results to improve, but as a morale booster – his very presence would lift the whole squad. He wasn't going to be rushed back, though; further injuries could be risked just to get him back playing. The club also had to look at the future and the worse-case scenario, next season without Jack and another injury would jeopardise that and risk any possible transfer if Villa were still in the Championship.

The question is, do miracles happen?

Chapter 6

'CAPTAIN JACK' TO THE RESCUE

Making Jack captain was a masterstroke.

Villa fans were looking for a miracle to save their season and looking at the return of Jack for the upcoming home game against Derby County as the catalyst for a change of fortunes; it would be the last throw of the dice, the last chance to salvage an average season. During the week leading up to his possible return it was touch and go, with the medical team 50/50 on whether they would give the green light or keep him on the treatment table. However, Jack sparked excitement among the fans when he Tweeted a picture of himself in action with the words, "Monday motivation." There was one shining light in the darkness; the three-month lay-off allowed Jack to improve his upper-body strength as he threw himself into some serious gym work at Bodymoor Heath; that picture showed he had been working on his muscles.

Villa looked to be some way adrift off the race for a top six finish, but a big win against Derby would at least keep their hopes alive a little longer. It was no coincidence that losing Jack for those three months led to a dip in form for Villa, but as soon as it looked as though he was fit to play again there seemed to be a different atmosphere around Villa Park.

With club captain James Chester out for the rest of the season, the role of captain had been given to a number of the Villa players, but with the news of Jack's return, Villa manager Dean Smith made a surprise decision that even the most ardent Villa fan would have been hard pushed to have dreamt up.

Dean Smith announced a day before the game that he had made the bold decision to make Jack club captain. When I first heard the news, my initial impression was of shock, not in a negative way, but I remember thinking to myself, "Wow, what a great decision", in fact, it was a decision I would have probably made myself if I was in the manager's boots, because it made complete sense. To those who were distant from the club, it was probably a mysterious, probably an unwise decision on Smith's part and a gamble maybe, but in hindsight it was a decision that would change the whole complexion of the season.

'Super Jack' was back - and now he was 'Captain Jack'!

Every football fan wants at least one player in his team to be the embodiment of their club, someone they can relate to and for Villa fans at that moment, it was Jack Grealish. Not only a Villa fan himself, but he came up through the ranks from a very young age, so automatically the fans will buy into it. What better person could Dean Smith have picked to become captain, other than Jack? For him, it must have been beyond all his wildest dreams and it must have meant so much to him.

For a 24-year-old to be given the captain's armband at a club as big as Aston Villa is remarkable in itself, and testament to the faith Dean Smith had in him.

The role of team captain has the potential to be the most challenging and most rewarding role of all for a football player. Maybe the role has been undermined in recent times, but it still holds some weight and no team can operate without a leader. When a manager appoints the captain, they need to consider a number of qualities in that player. A captain of a football club, especially a big club like Aston Villa, who's fans demand results, good football and for their players to respect the badge. He must be competent as a player, inspire confidence in their team-mates, be able to evaluate the game plan and the ability to change the game if need be. The player must also be able to handle the pressure, make tactical decisions and communicate effectively, not only with his manager, but his team-mates as well and also with the referee.

It must be worth noting that each captain is different; there isn't one set standard for a captain to follow, and they all have very different personalities. Two diverse examples in recent times would be: David Beckham who was a great player and led by example but wasn't the most vocal of skippers, and someone like John Terry, who was a leader of people, vocal and who demanded respect from his troops, more in the mould of an 'old-fashioned' captain.

What type of captain would Jack be?

If you look at how many foreign players there have been in the Premier League, and in particular those players who have been captains, how many of them felt an affinity to the club they were asked to lead? Of course, there are exceptions, like Vincent Kompany when he was Manchester City captain. You could tell what it meant to him to be their leader and he definitely had an affinity to the club. Ok, some may kiss the badge every now and again, but that doesn't mean anything nowadays – well maybe for five minutes it does? That's why making Jack Grealish captain was, in my opinion, the right thing to do, even though it was a left-field decision, but there was no one else for me. As a Villa fan, you know if and when Jack kisses the badge, he really means it. While there have been some very good foreign captains in the Premier League. A local lad lead the team out is something very special.

When you think about other players who have been the mainstay of the club in recent times, you automatically think of the likes of Steven Gerard at Liverpool or Mark Noble at West Ham. Players who the fans relate to and represent the very nature of their club. They both became captains and both would have done anything for their club. Handing Jack the captain's armband with 11 games of the 2018 - 2019 EFL Championship season and with Villa mid-table, it was definitely a masterstroke only someone who knew what it would mean to Jack would have done. Dean Smith, being a Villa fan himself, knew what it meant to Jack being asked to fulfil that role.

Having said that, all team captains must have the same traits to make them a good captain: be mentally strong, be an excellent communicator and self-confident. If you look into why Dean Smith made him captain, you can see the reasons behind his decision making - Jack has all the above traits in abundance.

It was no secret that the Villa squad at the time were almost dependant on Jack Grealish coming back into the side, and the poor results on the pitch while Jack was injured demonstrated that point. Smith must have looked around the dressing room and realised his importance. Coming back from injury and being made club captain must have given him a huge lift. Not that he needed it, because he is Villa through and through and he would have lifted his game anyway. It was evident that he's a big character in the dressing room and everyone responds to what he does out on the pitch.

So, how did Dean Smith break the news to Jack? "I remember the day I was named captain. In fact, I'll never forget it," Jack was quoted in saying to Ryan Grant in the 2020 League Cup Final matchday programme, "It was the day before the Derby game (2nd March 2019), I'd just come back from injury and I was in the physio room. I was with John McGinn and the manager walked in. We said, 'gaffer, who's going to be captain?' and he made us guess. We guessed a few names before he stopped me in my tracks and said, 'Jack, it's you, you're going to be captain. It's a hard feeling to describe. I remember calling my dad straight away, I was so excited and he filled up a little bit. I said I'd cherish every moment and I have; I'm a Villa fan and have been since I was a boy, so to be captain is a dream come true."

Those words from Jack says a lot about the passion he has for his boyhood club, and the pride of being made captain. Some people believe that certain things happen for a reason, and maybe making him captain at that key time in the season was one of those moments. The Villa manager explained he also looked at other players in the dressing room before making up his mind. Tommy Elphick, Glenn Whelan, Tyrone Mings all had leadership qualities and had a turn with the skipper's armband before, but I think there was only one name he was going to call upon.

Jack told AVTV, "The manager giving me the armband I felt like he trusted me and believed in me and it helped me on the pitch." Speaking about Dean Smith as a manager, Jack said, "He's just a perfect manager for me. He knows when to tell you if you're doing wrong or you're doing right, and he can have a joke with you as well. But for me, he's given me so much confidence and belief and he makes me feel like I'm the best player in the world. That helps me on the pitch. It's a pleasure playing for him."

After a three-month stretch out on the side-lines with injury, and his club not winning in the previous five games, the game against Derby County was a big moment in the career of Jack Grealish – and an important turning point in the season for Aston Villa. Before the home game with Derby County on 2nd March 2019, Villa were 13th in the Championship, with 45 points, eight points behind Bristol City in sixth place and had played a game more. Therefore, if you're a football romantic, you could say it was written in the stars that Jack would score one of the goals of the season that night at Villa Park. If you were a realist, you'd say the very talk of it would be just pie-in-the-sky.

But that's exactly what happened and the masterplan couldn't have gone any better, as Jack got on the scoresheet with a breath-taking fourth goal, which was a goal-of-the-season candidate in its own right. To score four goals before half-time is exceptional in any division, but when your backs are against the wall, it's even harder. Derby were simply blown away.

Suddenly, everything seemed rosy in the Villa Park garden.

Dean Smith told the AVFC website about Jack after the victory over Derby County, "He had a big smile on his face and it would have been a proud moment for him because, like me, he's a Villa fan and was brought up to be a Villa fan. To captain your team and score a goal like he did topped off a great day. For me, it was quite an easy decision. I had no doubts about giving it to Jack. I knew it wouldn't be a burden to him and that he would relish it – it's his club, he's a Villa fan. He's got a long-term contract at the club. When I came in, I said how I wanted him to lead us into the Premier League. I think he can do that. He's the future of this football club. He's a really good professional as well, and I felt if I didn't give it to him it could be overlooking the leadership qualities I know he has. He leads by example in the way he plays. I felt making him captain could enhance those qualities."

Those words from Dean Smith say an awful lot about the qualities Jack possesses and the kind of person he his, on and off the pitch. That's why I don't think any other manager would have made that decision at that moment in time. Dean Smith made it at just the right time, and you have to give him a lot of credit for that. Sure, it could be seen as a 'gamble', but put yourself in Dean Smith's shoes, he needed to do something different if his team were going to make one last push for the play-offs.

Jack was substituted on the 70th minute of that game against Derby and came off to a standing ovation from the 37,273 crowd, which was testament to the contribution he'd made that evening.

What happened in his comeback game on 2nd March was the start of quite simply, an unbelievable time in the history of Aston Villa; the weeks that followed that battering of the Rams was not only simply magical, but it was also unprecedented in the club's history. It was also a (another) miracle.

That result alone was enough to get the tongues wagging and the Villa fans dreaming. Could we...? Surely not?"

Up next was another mouth-watering local derby at St Andrews against Birmingham City. If you thought the Derby County game was nerve-tingling, then this game was something even more remarkable, and in part not for the right reasons.

If there wasn't enough ill-feeling between Birmingham City fans and Aston Villa fans, it was fuelled even more so when Birmingham midfielder, Maikel Kieftenbeld's late challenge on the Villa captain, in only the fourth minute, set the tone for the rest of the game. The noisy home fans were on Jack's back from that incident and they suggested he had overdramatised his fall to the ground. Six minutes later, when Jack was charging up the field to chase down a ball from a throw-in close to the corner flag, Jack walked away with his back towards the Blues fans. With Jack caught off-guard, he was attacked from behind by a spectator (I'll chose not to call him a 'fan'), who somehow evaded the line of orange and yellow jacketed stewards to make his way onto the pitch. As a football supporter, I was stunned watching this incident unfold in front of my own eyes.

Both sets of players confronted the thug involved and dragged him back towards the stands and into police custody. Jack was unhurt, fortunately for everyone concerned, because it could have been a lot worse. What if the idiot had a knife in his hand?

It was an absolute disgrace! There's a place in football for passion and exuberance, but there's no place for thuggery behaviour like that.

As everyone on the pitch, in the crowd and watching at home were trying to make head and tail of the event and the chaos that erupted around him, the Villa skipper merely dusted himself off, shrugged off the incident, adjusted his (mini) shin pads and got back to his feet. To Jack's great credit, and this shouldn't be overlooked, he didn't seem fazed by the incident. Few could argue that his concentration must have been thrown but he was eager to get going again.

Fate usually comes into play when things like that happen in football matches, or in life for that matter, and it appeared that way, when in the 67th minute, Alan Hutton went on a marauding run and Jack netted the winning goal as he crashed home a left-footed shot which sparked wild celebrations amongst the 2,074 travelling Villa fans. A minute later, Jack got booked for jumping over the barrier into the crowd. Both sides had chances, but Villa had the cutting edge and saw out the victory. It was an ugly affair, as you'd probably expect in a local derby, with both sides having three players booked, but the game will be remembered for the wrong reasons.

After the game, Dean Smith couldn't speak highly enough of his captain, "Jack Grealish is a mature lad, and he responded well. There was only one way to answer that and that was to pop up with a winner like he did. I'm really proud of the way he handled it. He only came off as he was knackered, cramping up. It was a scrappy derby in difficult conditions but we were the better team in the second half and deserved to win. A lot has been made of the Birmingham City team spirit, but we showed a lot of spirit ourselves. Conditions were tough but we put in a gritty performance."

That is one game Jack Grealish won't forget in a hurry, that's for sure. If Jack seemed unnerved by the attack while it was going on, he was even more so after the event, as he told talkSPORT, "I couldn't care less that he had done it; I genuinely could not care, and that is honestly from my heart. I don't know if he got egged on by people, and at the end of the day he done it. I was just thinking in my head, 'just please you've got to score the winner, and it was just perfect, 1 – 0 and me getting the winner. It was just meant to be. After the game I was so, so happy. My mum so, so upset thinking what the guy could have had on him – he could have anything on him, but I wasn't bothered one bit. At the end of the day if that's what he wanted to do then he can do it, but I was so happy to have scored the winner."

Listening to that interview with talkSPORT, really tells you what great mental attributes Jack has developed in order to handle incidents like that and think nothing of it, and the winning goal in that game was the only thing on his mind. It was a refreshing interview and respect to Jack for how he handled that uncomfortable situation.

A few days after the game had ended, the thug who was arrested for attacking Jack appeared in Birmingham Magistrates Court and admitted running on the pitch and assaulting the Villa captain. He was jailed for 14 weeks, banned from football stadiums for 10 years and ordered to pay Jack £100 compensation for the pain, shock and discomfort caused by the unprovoked attack. He was also banned from St Andrew's for life. In the hearing, the defendant said he wasn't intoxicated and did it as a 'joke'. If that was his version of a joke then the guy has a warped sense of humour! He said he was remorseful of the incident, but that didn't make up for the disgraceful behaviour. His solicitor said after the hearing, "My client doesn't seek to justify his behaviour at all. He has brought shame upon himself and his family...and the football club he has supported since he was a child. He apologises to Aston Villa and in particular Jack Grealish for his terrible behaviour. He cannot explain what came over him. He is certainly remorseful today."

The court also heard a statement prepared by Jack, which stated, "I cannot help but feel how lucky I was in this incident. It could have been so much worse had the supporter had some sort of weapon."

The three points took Villa closer to the top-six, only four points off Derby in sixth place. It had turned out to be a defining, and eventful eight days in the history of Aston Villa, and the short career of Jack Grealish.

By the time Blackburn Rovers visited Villa Park on the 30th March, the evidence of Jack's presence in the Villa team was there for all to see. They had recorded four back-to-back victories, two at home and two away, and under the watchful eye of England manager, Gareth Southgate, Jack was becoming the player to watch. However, it was Villa's on-loan striker Tammy Abraham who was knocking in most of the goals, as he scored again, for the 18th time at Villa Park to help his side record another win. Dean Smith summed it up to BBC Radio WM, "These players have got a newfound resilience where, even when they're 1 - 0 up, they're confident and feel like no one is going to go and score goals against them and break them down. It's taken a mistake for Blackburn to score and that's a credit to the players and how they're playing at the moment. We've had a fabulous March and getting that win puts us in a good position and some momentum towards April and May, now."

After another victory away to Steve Bruce's Sheffield Wednesday, Jack found the net again with the winner against struggling Rotherham at the New York Stadium. It was a game of penalties, three in all. Early in the first half, Jack was brought down in the area by Clark Robertson, but Tammy Abraham's penalty was turned around the post by the 'keeper. The second penalty was scored by Rotherham's Will Vaulks on 36 minutes, after Tyrone Mings handled the ball in the area and was red-carded. Then just after half-time, substitute Jonathan Kodjia equalised from the spot for his first League goal of 2019 after Rotherham's Semi Ajayi was punished for handling in the area. After a further three minutes, Villa were ahead. A slick run by Jack put the ball out to Ahmed Elmohamady, who returned the ball to his captain for him to tuck the ball away from 12 yards - his fifth goal of the season.

That result sent Villa into fifth place. The impossible was still alive.

Another home win against fellow contenders, Bristol City saw Tammy Abraham score his 24th goal of the season in a Villa shirt. That game against the Robins broke a sequence of seven games that Jack appeared in since coming back from his injury as he was left out due to illness. However, it showed everyone that the team could still win without their talisman, even if it was only going to be for one game. Dean Smith explained, "Jack's just ill, he had a fever.

When I spoke to him this morning he was devastated. He couldn't even go upstairs to take a shower. Hopefully the monkey's off our back now, we've got a win without Jack Grealish in the team."
Next up were Bolton Wanderers, who were one defeat from relegation. With the game goalless at half-time, Villa claimed the lead just two minutes into the second-half when Tammy Abraham crossed to the far post for Jack to head home. Ten minutes later Jack turned provider to Abraham, collecting a pass by John McGinn and setting up Abraham to head home and become the first Villa player to score 25 League goals in a season (albeit in a lower league) since Andy Gray did it in the 1976 – 1977 season. Villa were four points behind West Bromwich Albion in fourth place and with three games to go and were odds' on to confirm a place in the play-offs. Bolton were relegated to League One and in doing so, Villa had equalled their club record from 1910 of nine straight wins in the League.

That 109-year record was broken by a solitary Jonathan Kodjia goal in the 30th minute of the home game against Millwall, stabbing in El Ghazi's cross from close-range. That win meant Dean Smith's men had secured a place in the play-offs for the second successive year.

It was a quite remarkable turnaround for them, and not to put a finer point on it, the main factor of the change in fortunes was the re-emergence of Jack Grealish, although you've got to give the whole squad credit for their efforts during those 10 games. Only a draw in the penultimate game of the season against Leeds and defeat at home to promoted Norwich dampened the spirits, but it was a marvellous achievement, nonetheless. It's worth mentioning the bizarre events during the Leeds game, where there was nothing riding on the game for either side; Leeds had blown their chances of automatic promotion and both clubs had already qualified for the play-offs. It was a heated affair, as ever with Leeds, but tempers were lost in the 72nd minute when chaos reigned on the pitch. Leeds initially opted to play on following a challenge by Leeds defender, Liam Cooper, which left Villa striker Jonathan Kodjia on the floor, before Tyler Roberts then appeared to be ready to put the ball out for a throw-in. However, Roberts had other ideas and instead passed the ball forward to Klich and, with the Villa defence flat-footed, although offside, he was allowed to run on, cut inside and curl a low right-foot shot just inside the post. In the aftermath, El Ghazi was sent off for an alleged elbow on Leeds striker Patrick Bamford, who dropped to the floor like a sack of potatoes, holding his face despite no apparent contact. It was one of those 'what happened next' moments, and hardly anybody would get the answer. It was an astonishing scene, Leeds boss Marcelo Bielsa ordered his players to allow Villa to equalise, and Albert Adomah was allowed to run through to score, almost unchallenged, into an unguarded net.

Have you ever seen anything like that before? Respect to Marcelo Bielsa for 'ordering' his team to concede a goal.

If the unprovoked attack on Jack Grealish wasn't bizarre enough, then Marcelo Bielsa's 'fair-play' moment probably topped it. Of course, Dean Smith praised his opposite number for his sportsmanship. Who knows if he'd have done the same if the result had anything riding on it, but fair play to him none-the-less.

Incidentally, Dean Smith made five changes including John McGinn and Tammy Abraham and chose to rest Jack for the final game of the season at home to Norwich, who were handed the League Championship trophy after the game.

That dip in form during the bleak winter months when Jack was injured was no coincidence after all, and it doesn't take a genius to realise what an impact Jack Grealish made to the side, merely by his presence and moreover, his skill and influence on and off the pitch. Manager, Dean Smith summed it up, "If you had asked me 11 games ago would we go and win the next 10, I would have thought you were a little bit crackers. The turning point was half-time at Stoke when I got into the players and we have been excellent since then. I don't think until I look back on it I will realise what we have actually done because my focus is still on getting promoted. This is a historic, great football club and to be the first manager to have achieved it is something special, but we want to continue it."

During that winning run, the friendship between Jack and his midfield partner, John McGinn developed and the two, who were similar ages and had similar interests started dining out together every Thursday and it became some sort of 'bromance' ritual. McGinn told the Telegraph, "A lot of the lads have got kids and their

Thursday nights are taken up. But we go out and get some food and it just started being a wee superstition and it's carried on. Jack is one of the best players I've played with. He's comfortably the best in the league. He just glides with the ball, he's comfortable with both feet and he gets kicked about all the time, but I've got no doubt in my mind he will be an England player one day. Everyone gets the perception that he's some sort of bad boy but he's a hard worker and he's been a great leader for us over the past months or ten weeks."

Of course, nothing had been achieved at that point, qualifying for the play-offs was a good start, but the most important task was getting the club back in the Premier League.

There was a six-day break before the first of the two-legged play-off semi-finals against local rivals West Bromwich Albion - it was to prove no easy path to Wembley for Villa. In front of an almost full Villa Park, Dwight Gayle spoilt the first-half with the opening goal from a header in 16th minute. However, the half-time team talk did the home side some good as they took the lead with two goals inside three minutes with a quarter of the game to go. Conor Hourihane's superb 25-yard shot levelled the score, then a Tammy Abraham penalty after Jack went down in the area turned the game in Villa's favour. The tipping point came late on when Albion's goal-scorer, Dwight Gayle was sent off for sliding into Villa 'keeper, Jed Steer, meaning he would miss the second-leg.

Villa took a one-goal advantage to The Hawthorns a few days later. It proved to be a tight affair, with Craig Dawson opening the scoring on the half-hour to level the tie, but the game fizzled out and went to extra-time and eventually penalties. Of course, our man Jack netted his penalty to make it 3 – 1 to Villa as he sent the 'keeper the wrong way. The penalty shoot-out was close from the first to last, with Villa coming out on top by 4 – 3 and sending their fans into dreamland, "It was a tough game and the crowd made it like that. It was a good game but we ended up worthy winners," Jack told Sky Sports.

Villa were in the final again, for the second time in consecutive seasons the dream was on.

Chapter 7

BACK IN THE BIG TIME

Jack's back where he belongs.

Aston Villa 2 Derby County 1

Aston Villa's three-year exile from the Premier League was over. The day belonged primarily to Dean Smith, but also to Villa's heroic captain, Jack Grealish, who once again showed why he is so special.

Jack's captaincy and subsequent contribution to the team since his comeback certainly turned out to be a masterstroke by Dean Smith, "Boy, the kid has matured," he said. There is a cliché often associated with life which goes, 'cometh the hour, cometh the man', and it was exactly that for Jack Grealish on that sunny May afternoon.

Watching Jack play live in that Final, watching how he handled the pressure during that 90 minutes, and indeed the previous three months of being captain. This must have changed some people's perception of Jack Grealish in a positive way. Being in the Championship, he was somewhat off the radar, but that final was the pedestal he needed to raise his profile on to the national stage. I don't think he'd had the plaudits he deserved and I don't think people, other than Villa fans, thought he was the 'real deal'.

Dean Smith obviously had a special bond and connection with him and has helped him transform his career. From being a 17-year-old who was in the media for the wrong reasons to being the most gifted English player of his generation is certainly something to be proud of. "A lot of people's perceptions are him lying in a road when he was 17 or 18. He was thrust into the limelight as a young kid, but boy the kid has matured," Dean Smith told The Telegraph.

It wasn't just Jack's contribution that was the key to Villa's revitalisation during the latter part of the season. Jack clearly went for superstition over style, because a pair of white boots also played a part in the change in fortunes. When he came back from injury, he scored that wonder goal against Derby and continued to wear the same pair of boots, which at the time were new and they soon became his 'lucky boots'. By the time of the final, they were battered and thread bare, but his 'lucky boots' served him well and they held up long enough to see the job through, "I came back from injury. I got a few goals, and I got a few assists and thought these were my lucky boots, I had to keep them, and I'm not even superstitious," Jack told Sky Sports.

The final itself didn't just mean a lot to the club, it meant a lot to Jack, who would certainly have left Villa had they lost at Wembley, "I'm absolutely speechless. It's a dream come true for me. I started the season not even thinking I was going to be a Villa player and ten months on I am here now. I'm the captain and we are back in the Premier League. Honestly, the best day of my life – I can't explain it," he told talkSPORT.

According to his father, Kevin, he asked Jack to give him his medal when he went with the team after the final, "I put it round my neck and went round to the hotel getting as many children as I could to have their photograph taken with it."

Once the celebrations had died down and everyone had got their breath back, Tottenham and other clubs had turned the attention onto other players. Having signed a five-year extension back in September 2018 under the previous manager, Steve Bruce, the Villa board moved quickly to secure the captain's services for a reported £100,000-a-week contract, activating a (reported) clause in his previous deal on the 26th July 2019. It was thought that his previous deal included a £60 million buyout clause – luckily that wasn't required. I would imagine that new deal included an even bigger buyout clause?

****

Season 2019 – 2020

For someone as young as Jack, he'd been through quite a lot since he made his Premier League debut in 2015. It has taken a lot of determination and application to get him through it all. He spoke to AVTV before the start of the 2019 – 2020 season about his career to date, "I feel like I've been around forever. I feel like it's the perfect time for myself to come back into the Premier League; maybe before I may have been a bit young – it may have all come to me a bit too soon. I'm ready now to showcase my talent in the toughest league in the world."

Thinking back on the last season, Jack said, "The whole of last season was a bit weird, full of ups and downs. At the start of the season, I didn't even think I was going to be here. If I'm honest, for the first two months I wasn't nowhere near where I should have been. Steve Bruce then got the sack and Dean Smith come in, he spoke to me, told me how he wants me to play and when he came in, it gave me a bit of a new lease of life really, on the pitch. I was playing with an injury then for five or six weeks and obviously I got my scan results back and it was way worse than I thought. So, I was out for three months; it was tough watching the boys and they didn't do too well. When I came back in all I wanted to do was to help the team."

The rest was history.

Aston Villa were celebrating their 145th year in existence and were back in the Premier League after a three-year exile. It was Dean Smith's first season as a Premier League manager, and he was relishing the challenge. As for Jack Grealish, he was as excited as a child in a sweet shop.

The club seemed 'different' to what it was three years previously; the staff, players and fans were all together and everyone was happier – there seemed like there was a camaraderie within the squad. It seemed unified at last, and Jack felt that change, "It comes from getting promoted last season. As soon as we went on that 10-game winning streak there was an instant bond between the players and the fans, especially, which is always nice - the fans play such a big part. There's so much positivity around the place and everyone is just looking forward to the season starting because we feel like we can have a good season."

In his last season as a Premier League player, he was still finding his feet as a person and as a professional footballer, let alone a top-flight player. He'd only scored one goal in the top-flight, but what a goal it was, against Leicester City on 13th September 2015. Fast-forward three years and Jack Grealish was becoming the player everyone thought he could be.

Dean Smith wanted to keep the spine of the successful team together, and that he did. With all the talk of Jack's new contract being secured right at the start of the pre-season, the Villa board did most of their transfer business early, bringing in Wesley Moraes from Belgium club Brugge for a record transfer fee of £22m, Matt Targett from Southampton for £11.5m, Ezri Konsa from Brentford for £12m and Douglas Luiz from Manchester City for £15m, to name but a few. They also secured last seasons' loanees Anwar El Ghazi (undisclosed), Kortney Hause (£3m) and Tyrone Mings for £20m on permanent deals. The spending was big and the quality was even bigger. A total of 12 players were drafted in before the 1st August deadline and over £120m spent. Up to 20 players were released, many on free transfers. Unfortunately, Tammy Abraham, who scored 25 league goals in the campaign, ended his loan spell and went back to Chelsea to fight for his place.

Of concern was that only five of the squad had previously played in the Premier League, so it was going to be a tough season adjusting to the new league. All the players were looking forward to playing at the big stadiums, like Anfield, Old Trafford and The Emirates.

However, it seemed like Christmas for the Villa fans, who were in for a treat, well on paper anyway.

Even though the new Villa board had put their money where their mouth was during the close season, nobody at Aston Villa FC were under any illusions it was ever going to be an easy ride for their newly promoted club, however big a club it was.

Villa had a good pre-season, winning all their games, but they count for nothing come the opening fixture of the season. Ironically, the opening game for Jack and his new team was against Tottenham Hotspur at their state-of-the-art new stadium. It could have been oh, so different for Jack had he chose to sign for Spurs after the 2017 – 2018 EFL Championship Play-Off Final defeat to Fulham, "It just had to be that one, didn't it? I'm looking forward to it. It's the perfect game to get us started and if we can go there and get a win or draw, who knows, that will set us on our way." Jack also told AVTV before the opening fixture, "I know the philosophy of the manager, he'll want nothing else but to win the game."

Dean Smith told Jack he wanted more goals from his midfield, and that included himself and John McGinn. After nine minutes you'd have thought Spurs were the newly promoted side and a John McGinn goal shook the home side, and for the first 70 minutes of the game in fact. However, as soon Tottenham made substitutions, the game changed on its head and resulted in three goals in the last 15 minutes for the home side and gave the visitors a lesson in clinical finishing.
Welcome to the Premier League!

By mid-September Villa were languishing in the bottom three but Dean Smith had faith in Jack and his team to spark their season into life and push Villa up the league. It had been a frustrating start to the season, with just one win against Everton in four games. Jack had performed to his usual high standard and remained a key player, as Smith told the Telegraph, "There will be more to come from Jack. He wants to get better. You end up sometimes dragging him off the training ground because he wants to get better. It's a massive plus in his favour. Jack's a football person. He will train all day and go and find a room somewhere and fall asleep. Then he'll wake up and go and do a gym session, that's how he is. He's that sort of character - I'm surprised his girlfriend is still with him! He'll go back home, and he'll be watching football as well. He's a football nut. Jack and John McGinn were probably our most influential players last season and to expect them to be as influential in the Premier League is asking a little bit too much straightaway. But they are getting better and better, that's for sure."

It was clear from watching Villa that Smith wanted Jack to play further up the field and to run at the opposition and hurt them on the break and that was demonstrated positively in the away game at Selhurst Park; however, it also showed Villa's weakness of conceding sloppy goals. To make matters worse, Trézéguet was sent off just after the half-time break for a second bookable offence and it got worse for Villa when Jack was booked for alleged diving just before Henri Lansbury's goal was disallowed right on the stroke of full-time. That game seemed to set the tone for the season.

It wasn't until the away game at Carrow Road in early October that everything seemed to click into place. With Jack effectively playing as a number 10 in a front three, it paid off in spectacular fashion against fellow newly promoted club, Norwich City. It was the game that Jack Grealish became a Premier League player and his performance that day must have alerted England manager, Gareth Southgate into considering him for a call-up. Simply put, Norwich were blown away and Jack was involved in everything that happened. With only four points on the board, Villa tore into a weak Norwich defence and were 2 – 0 up through Wesley on the half-hour. After the break, Jack got on the scoresheet, finishing off a fine attacking move and ended up having a hand in all five goals scored on the day.

It was a long time coming but Dean Smith's tactical change brought dividends and likewise, in the next game at home against Brighton in front of an almost full-house, Jack was on the scoresheet again, with his fourth goal in all competitions, overturning Adam Webster's opening goal. Matt Targett scored the winner deep into injury time, finishing off a Grealish cross to seal the win.

Villa were catapulted into 11th place with 11 points from nine games and suddenly things looked on the up until defeats to Manchester City, Liverpool and Wolves brought them crashing back down to earth. Jack was replaced late on at The Etihad with a calf injury which eventually ruled him out of the games against Liverpool and Wolves – how they needed him too. It soon became apparent that playing without Jack in the side was going to be tough, if they didn't need reminding.

However, he was soon back, and his class was highlighted in the next game, a tough away fixture at Old Trafford. It took just 11 minutes for Villa to take the lead when Jack sidestepped Pereira with ease in the penalty area before bending a stunning shot into the top corner. Dean Smith stood and admired the shot, "It was a super goal, but it is what I have come to expect from him." It most certainly was a contender for 'goal of the season'. Villa had put in a dogged performance against a below par United side who couldn't hold on to a lead. Tyrone Mings sealed a point in the 66th minute with a volley but only after United had come from behind to lead 2 – 1 going into the closing 20 minutes. That point moved Villa into 15th place.

December proved a tough month, until Boxing Day when a narrow victory over Norwich gave light relief, following four straight defeats. During those losses Jack managed to get on the scoresheet twice, even though his goals proved futile. The worst performance came at Villa Park against high-flying Leicester City, in a game billed as the match-up between two of England's best midfielders, Jack Grealish and James Maddison. Jack gave Villa some hope by scoring just before the break to make it 2 – 1 to the visitors, but the second half was forgetful, a collapse ensued and nothing good can be said about that game.

On New Years' Day, Jack showed why he was proving to be the most wanted player in the Premier League as he produced, arguably his most influential performance of the season away at Burnley. It was an all-round brilliant performance and the opposite to the previous game away at Watford, the whole team were woeful. It started in the 12th minute, when Wesley's heel was proved offside by VAR to cancel out Jack's effort, but the big striker made amends when he opened the scoring in the 27th minute. Jack then doubled Villa's lead four minutes before the half-time whistle with a powerful strike into the top corner. Villa were all over the hosts, but they had a lifeline in the 80th minute when Chris Wood headed home but Villa hung on for the last ten minutes. The win moved Villa up the table to 16th; however, the win proved costly as both Wesley and goalkeeper, Tom Heaton were stretchered off with nasty-looking injuries that ruled both out for the rest of the season..... and longer.

After conceding six against Manchester City, Villa needed a decent result to get them out of the bottom three. After going 1 – 0 down at Brighton after 38 minutes, Jack scored one of the goals of the season in a 1 – 1 draw at the Amex Stadium. He'd already scored eight goals in all competitions by then, but that goal against the Seagulls was probably the best. With the game drifting away from Villa in the second half, Jack showed a moment of quality to control Douglas Luiz's pass, shimmy away from the defender before firing beyond Mat Ryan for his ninth goal of the season. His manager described the goal, "It's a super ball and a super strike from Jack. He's in great goalscoring form; he's in great form full stop and it just shows the sort of player he is."

Jack admitted to AVTV that he prefers to score goals rather than assists, although he likes to help create goals as well, "As a midfield player it's nice to assist your striker, but the goals I scored (during the 2019 – 2020 season) I don't think there's much that beats getting on the scoresheet. I had a few nice ones, where you're celebrating in front of the away fans, at Brighton for example – I loved that goal."

The League Cup had been a good distraction from the Premier League for Villa throughout the season and a two-legged semi-final tie with local rivals Leicester City proved invaluable to the suffering fans. A hard-fought draw in the first leg at the King Power Stadium was followed by a classic cup night at Villa Park. The stadium was rocking throughout a pulsating match. Again, it was down to the captain, who led from the front and pulled all the strings, his neat flick to Matty Targett gave the home side the lead in the 12th minute with a thunderous low shot that was fired between Schmeichel's legs.

However, Villa were indebted to goalkeeper, Orjan Nyland, who made a string of astonishing saves to deny the Foxes. Going into the 90th minute, the score was 1 – 1 with both sides pushing for the winner until, that was, Trézéguet produced a decisive finish from a perfect cross from Elmohamady, three minutes into injury time to send his club into the final. There were wild scenes of jubilation when the whistle blew as hundreds of fans invaded the pitch.

Villa were on their way back to Wembley again; Jack was going to play on another big stage.

The season was proving to be a good one for Jack personally, and up until the League Cup Final, no other English player in the Premier League had created more chances, and he'd also contributed with seven league goals himself.

Between the semi-final second leg and the final, Villa recorded three straight defeats in the league so there wasn't a lot of expectancy going into the Wembley final against Manchester City on 1st March 2020. It was Villa's first final since 2010, when they lost to Manchester United, and City's third successive League Cup final. Indeed, the class of the 2019 – 2020 Premier League champions was there for everyone to see and no-one watching that game could argue against their claims to the first piece of silverware of the season. As for Jack, he'd been to Wembley four times with Villa, with two wins and two defeats, but he was the man for the big occasion, "I love playing here," he told the League Cup Final matchday programme, "I'm lucky. Some players don't ever get this chance in their whole career. I love the big occasion. What's not to love? You're playing at Wembley in a major final with everyone watching."

Speaking about his time at Villa to date, he said, "This club is massive to me. I've been here since I was six and have done everything I ever dreamed of. I've played and scored in the Premier League, scored against Blues, captained the club, everything. Lifting a trophy would be right up there."

However, the game itself didn't turn out to be the dream Jack had hoped it would be. City controlled most of the game and led 2 – 1 at half-time. The second half was much of the same, although Villa almost took the game into extra-time as they showed some resilience late on. However, Jack couldn't perform any miracles or any sort of serious influence during a hard-fought contest. At full-time, the pain and disappointment on his face was plain to see.

Eight days after the cup final defeat, Villa crashed and burned yet again in the league against Leicester at the King Power Stadium. In what turned out to be the last football game in England before the COVID-19 national lockdown, Villa were given a lesson in clinical finishing as the Foxes struck four times without reply and Villa remained stuck in the relegation zone.

The (first) national lockdown ended all sporting activities for three months, but when the Premier League restarted on 17th June 2020, there was something missing from every stadium – the fans.

Villa effectively started their 'mini-season' again, a series of 10 games to save their Premier League status.

With four games to go, Villa were still stuck in the bottom three, well behind Watford in 17th place. However, it seemed that the lights had switched on when a Trézéguet double against Crystal Palace at Villa Park seemed to ignite the season at last. His brace claimed Villa's first league win since 21st January and moved them within four points of safety. It was a huge three points.

Another good performance at Goodison Park earned Villa a point towards safety. Five days later, with Villa in the bottom three, a home game against Arsenal was billed as a 'cup final' by Dean Smith, and Jack was definitely the one you wanted in your side for the big games. What we didn't know before that game was the state of Jack's mind, given the season had been delayed due to COVID-19, the game against the Gunners was on 21st July, normally a time when players were preparing for the following season, but in the middle of summer, Villa needed to win or face the drop – and Jack was apparently still in two minds about his long-term future.

The game couldn't have gone any better, with another Trézéguet stunner sealing a fine win against Arsenal and pushed Villa outside the relegation zone at last. Jack put in another huge shift and was voted man-of-the-match against Arsenal, inspiring his team mates to a crucial victory which moved his team above Watford on goal difference and into 17th place.

Villa's last game was away to West Ham and they needed a win - providing Watford didn't win by a margin two or more goals greater than they did – Dean Smith's team would secure another season in the top-flight, having spent much of it in the bottom three. Their fate was back in their own hands.

The London Stadium was the venue for Villa's most important game of the season against West Ham, and what a game it turned out to be. If the season hinged on one game, that was it. It wasn't quite 'win or bust' but depending on other results, it could have turned out that way. It is said that the big players turn up for the big games, and Jack, being Villa's biggest player, was energetic throughout the game, without being spectacular but he came alive with six minutes of the game (and the season) to go. With the score at 0 – 0 until the 84th minute, up pops 'Super Jack', dancing through the West Ham defence into the penalty area as if they weren't there but saw his shot deflected wide, then found space on the edge of the box before firing his shot into the net to score his 10th goal of the season in all competitions. The Villa players surrounded Jack and he ran towards the bench with delight. That should have been the end of the matter; however, the Hammers struck back straight away and gave Villa a scare until other results went Villa's way to end the rollercoaster season.

The season was over, and Villa had escaped the drop; defeat at the London Stadium would have sealed their relegation for sure. After the game, wild scenes of celebration from the Villa players and staff were held on the pitch in front of the empty stadium. Dean Smith told the BBC, "When Jack scores you think 'That's it we're safe' but a deflection made it a little bit nervous, but we saw it out well. I'm immensely proud and I've said that in the dressing room. We now look like Premier League players."

After that game, Jack spoke to AVTV about his feelings, especially the moment after he scored the opening goal which he thought was the winner, "I was due a goal. The manager said to me after every game in lockdown, 'you aren't going to go all these 10 games without a goal', so he was right. Obviously it took a while for the last one, but as soon as the goal went in I thought that's it now, we've done it, but two minutes later Yarmolenko cuts in, has a shot and it deflects off me and goes in. At the time I was a bit on edge for the last few minutes. During the last seven or eight minutes I wasn't too bad; I think the game kind of died out after that. They didn't go crazy for it, but nor did we. We were happy with a point. But it was a day to remember and something I'll never forget."

After scoring that goal, Jack was famously pictured with his fingers in his ears, possibly referring to all the speculation surrounding him.

Talking about how the team completely turned the season around during those last 10 games, Jack credited the whole team. There seemed to be a newfound solidity, especially in defence, "Before lockdown our defensive record wasn't the best, we conceded a lot of chances, but during lockdown we had countless number of Zoom sessions, set-piece meetings, we had done so much I honestly can't explain how much we done and it all paid off. Defensively, we were probably one of the best after lockdown and it all come together."

It seemed the whole team became a tighter nit group after lockdown, which was testament to Dean Smith and the coaching staff. Not only that, but Jack also explained that the whole group seemed to bond during that period and that certainly helped get the team playing better than they did before the break, "That's what the gaffer tried to install into us a bit."

With the season ending on a high, Jack was not only named Aston Villa Players' Player of the Year, but also the Aston Villa Supporters' Player of the Year.

****

Season 2020 - 2021

As with the previous two or three seasons, the Villa board were again primed to deal with rumours linking Jack with a move away, despite survival on the last day of the season. However, they could, thankfully, negotiate from a slightly different position, a position of strength rather than weakness – they were still a top-flight club, cash-rich and ready for the 2020 – 2021 season.

This time, it wasn't Tottenham the media were talking about, it was Manchester City and Manchester United, who were supposedly in for him. As for Jack, he kept out of the limelight and spent some of the summer getting fit for the season and he told AVTV, "Towards the end of the summer I was in Dubai training with Ross Barkley and I come back at the start of July and I felt as fit as I'd ever felt really."

While all the transfer deals were going ahead behind the scenes, Jack ignored all the talk in the media about supposed interest from the Manchester clubs by pledging his future to Villa by signing a new five-year contract, said to be worth around £125,000 a week, a club record. This, after Jack had made his belated international debut for England against Denmark. It was a massive boost for Villa, who quite frankly, could not have survived the previous campaign without their talisman midfielder and captain.

The impact of COVID-19 on football clubs' finances took their toll and it played into the hands of Villa, who were able to quickly tie up the deal with Jack, without any sort of negotiations from any other club ever materialising, because it was merely paper talk at the end of the day. Jack was reportedly quoted as saying, "It was the stuff of dreams" and a relief to have signed again for his boyhood club, revealing he held talks with Dean Smith, Christian Purslow and Nassef Sawiris over the deal on FaceTime, just before Villa's pre-season friendly against Manchester United at Villa Park on 13th September 2020 and suggested to the Birmingham Mail, "Four or five days ago, I genuinely didn't know where I was going to be starting the season, that's how intense it was." Jack also told the Telegraph, "It's been difficult for me being a Villa fan my whole life and being captain, not knowing where I was going to be over the summer. The hopes the owners have got for the club was a massive factor in me deciding to stay. Last season we finished 17th after spending a lot of money and we were probably lucky to stay in the league. But the ambition and drive the owners have got, bringing some brilliant players in, is something that we need. I believe in the project that they want to go forward with. Now I can have my head straight before the start of the season. I didn't want to be playing a few games for Villa and then moving, so I'm just so glad it's all sorted. The owners have made it very clear to me how ambitious they are and how they want to build Aston Villa. There are exciting times ahead and I am very glad to be part of it."

Jack also told the Aston Villa website that it was a "nice problem to have" having a lot of attention on him from other clubs, "if you've been linked with them you know you've been doing something well."

After the long chat with Christian Purslow, Dean Smith and the owner, Nassef Sawiris, Jack said he told his agent, Jonathan Barnett about his decision, that "my future is with Aston Villa," and that he believed in the project going forward. Whatever was said in the four-way FaceTime meeting it definitely persuaded Jack to be part of the future of the club, at least for another season. In a world where football agents seem to have a lot, if not too much, power that says a lot about Jack and his loyalty to his boyhood club. Jack said he wanted to repay the faith the board and manager have shown in him and improve on the previous season.

Dean Smith played a major part in convincing his skipper that his future lay with Villa. When he was asked what was said to convince him to commit his future, Smith told the Birmingham Mail, "We just spoke about the ambitions of the football club. None of us were satisfied with finishing 17th in the Premier League the season before and how we wanted to improve. We gave Jack a little insight into the owner's vision of where we want to be as a club within the next three or four years and Jack was committed to that then."

Villa CEO, Christian Purslow, said, "Jack is an emblem of our owner's vision for Aston Villa. He joined our club as a local boy aged six and has developed into one of the country's finest players finally becoming a full England international last week. We are determined to build a top team around him and are delighted that he is extending his contract and committing himself to the club he loves."

During the shorter summer break, which wasn't the normal close season due to the disruption the COVID-19 lockdown caused, Villa splashed the cash like no other season, breaking their transfer record with the signing of striker, Ollie Watkins from Brentford for £28m, Matty Cash from Nottingham Forest for £14m, goalkeeper Emiliano Martínez for £20m from Arsenal and Bertrand Traoré for £17m from Lyon.

How much influence Jack had in the recruitment process, nobody knows, but it seems that some of the new lads coming in were familiar to Jack. Speaking to AVTV, Jack gave an insight into the dressing room and how he bonds with his teammates, "I like to have a good bond with them. When I first came into the first team, I had a great bond with Benteke when he was here, we used to bounce off each other and we loved playing with each other and I feel I had that with a few strikers. I had it with Wesley, actually. A lot of people probably won't believe it but we actually had a good relationship off the pitch, me and Wes. I'm sure I'll have that with Ollie."

The Villa board's work in the transfer window must have convinced Jack that those days of fighting relegation every season could be a thing of the past. Sawiris and Edens did not buy the club to be scrapping around the bottom three of the Premier League, so signing Jack up on a new long-term contract and the huge amount spent on quality players showed a huge statement of intent going into the new season.

Speaking to AVTV about the hopes for the season ahead, Jack was realistic about where he saw the team finish in the Premier League, "Everyone wants to build on what we did last season, and at the start of last season (2019 – 2020 season) we were probably aiming at finishing 12th or 14th but it doesn't always work out as you plan. Hopefully, this season (2020 – 2021 season) we can build on that, especially with Ollie (Watkins), Matty (Cash) and the squad we have here at the moment, I think we can aim higher, that is genuine. I think we have to look between 12th and 8th really. You've got to be realistic and go through stages; you're not going to finish 17th one season then finish 5th or 6th the next."

On a personal note, Jack spoke about his own targets, after scoring 10 goals in the last campaign, he was looking at improving on his own stats for the new season, "As an attacking player you've got to look at stats like that. I want to get goals; I want to get assists and if I'm doing that then I'm doing my job. I've also got into the England squads in the last few months so that's a big thing I want to improve on this season. I want to build on my numbers from last season, goals and assists and also get up the table with Villa."

The opening game of the season was an EFL League Cup win at Burton, where Jack celebrated signing his new contract by getting on the scoresheet with a fine late volley as Villa came from behind to win 3 – 1.

The Premier League season started about five or six weeks later than usual due to the previous (disrupted) season not finishing until July. Villa's opener was a home game against Sheffield United on 21st September, and they carried on their winning ways with a 1 – 0 victory courtesy of Ezri Konsa. Gareth Southgate was in the stands to watch Jack, along with other candidates like Konsa, Tyrone Mings and Ollie Watkins in preparation for naming his England squad for the games against Wales, Belgium and Denmark. Jack was the main focus of attention, after making his bow in the previous set of international fixtures.

The next three fixtures (including the Fulham game) all ended in wins for Villa and Jack played a pivotal part in all of them, as you'd expect. Gareth Southgate's number two, Steve Holland was at Craven Cottage to watch a one-sided game, especially in the first half, when Villa were 2 – 0 up in the space of 15 minutes. The first goal was as simple as they get, with John McGinn picking out Jack who slotted home after four minutes. Goals from Hourihane and Mings made the score 3 – 0 and there was no way back for Fulham. Jack was, again, Man of the Match with a classy display. Although it wasn't a bad-tempered affair, there were no less than nine bookings on either side.

On 30th September, Villa signed Ross Barkley from Chelsea on a season long loan. Everyone knows the talent he has and on his day, he's unplayable. However, not everyone was aware that Jack and Ross were good friends and Jack was a major influence in the club signing him. Jack told AVTV, "I was constantly texting him and it was actually before the Fulham game (on 28th September) that I texted him saying 'we've actually got a good side this year, if you're going to leave make sure you have us in mind. That night we played Fulham and beat them 3 – 0 and played really well and after that game he must have thought, 'maybe Jack was right'."

Ross Barkley duly signed two days after those texts and after that emphatic win at Craven Cottage.

Next up were Liverpool at Villa Park, in what can only be described as a one-in-a-million game, a game that no one could have ever predicted.

JACK NETS CITY'S FOURTH IN THE 6-3 CHAMPIONS LEAGUE
GROUP-STAGE WIN OVER RB LEIPZIG, 15 SEPTEMBER 2021

JACK GETS AWAY FROM
N'GOLO KANTE DURING THE
1-0 WIN AT STAMFORD BRIDGE
25 SEPTEMBER 2021

JACK CELEBRATES
WITH THE FANS AFTER
SCORING HIS FIRST CITY
GOAL IN THE 5-0 WIN
OVER NORWICH CITY
21 AUGUST 2021

Aston Villa 7 Liverpool 2

An Ollie Watkins double within the first 25 minutes shocked the opposition, and everyone watching at home. It looked interesting when Mo Salah grabbed a goal back on the half hour, but two more goals before half-time from Watkins and McGinn sent shivers down the spine of the Villa fans at home, and despair for the Liverpool fans. On 75 minutes it was 7 - 2, with the game looking as though any score was possible. Jack deservedly got his name on the scoresheet when his strike cannoned off Fabinho, making it 6 – 2, and he bagged his brace in the 75th minute when he was sent racing clean through and he dinked a smart finish past Adrián at his near post – sending Villa into dreamland. However, even though Jack was at the heart of everything that happened, the night belonged to Ollie Watkins, who scored his first three goals as a Premier League striker, and what a night he chose to do it.

AVTV spoke to Jack about the unbelievable win, "It was good. It would have been so much better if we had our fans there, but to beat the Champions 7 – 2 at Villa Park it will be something that will stay with us forever, especially the lads who were on the pitch at the time and it will live long in the memory of all the Aston Villa fans as well."

Dean Smith was almost as speechless as Jürgen Klopp after the game, "To be 4 - 1 up at half-time was surreal. To get a result and performance like that against an exceptional team takes something special." It must have been his proudest moment of his Premier League managerial career, if not his entire management career.

Liverpool manager, Jürgen Klopp, was seen on camera saying, "Wow!" to Dean Smith after the game. That just about summed up the night.

The Villa statistics in that game were as unbelievable as the score line:

11 shots on target
7 goals
30% possession

As for Jack's personal contribution he was directly involved in five of the seven goals:

3 Assists
2 goals

Liverpool's normally steadfast and tight defenders, Trent Alexander-Arnold and Joe Gomez were terrorised. Jack was cleverly and courageously urged by Dean Smith to focus on counterattacking rather than persistently chasing back and that was the key to the performance. The English Champions were torn apart and made Jack look more like Lionel Messi and gave him so much space on the left it was rather like the Liverpool defenders were pleading with Gareth Southgate to start the attacker for England. It was great to watch – if you were a Villa fan.

With three successive wins and Jack looking like the superstar every Villa fan always knew he was. The foundation was there to start a stellar campaign. Any thoughts of a predictable title race were dead and buried because of the random results the Premier League was dishing up.

The King Power Stadium hasn't always been a happy ground for Villa in recent years, but Ross Barkley grabbed his second goal in as many games to score the winner in injury time. What a season this was turning out to be – four wins out of four for Villa, the first time that had been achieved since 1930 – 1931 season. Incredible! As for Jack, he was on fire, fresh from his first England start against Wales, he was dictating the attacking play from the left wing as Villa began to control the game as the half wore on and was leading his side like a true captain. There was no stopping Villa in this sort of attacking form.

The next two games proved to be a lesson in complacency. Both Leeds and Southampton crushed Villa in back-to-back home fixtures and scored seven goals between them. The performance against Leeds was one we all would want to forget. Although a late comeback against the Saints almost finished in a draw, with Ollie Watkins making it 4 – 2 with a penalty three minutes into injury time and Jack scoring as late as seven minutes into injury time, but it was too little, too late and the visitors claimed their 4 – 3 victory.

Normal service was resumed at the Emirates, where Jack and his troops were truly unstoppable, and especially Ollie Watkins, who grabbed his fifth and sixth goals in seven games to inspire a 3 – 0 victory – and it could have been more. He was proving a handful and justifying he was worth the £22m price tag that Dean Smith had invested in him. Three away wins in a row without conceding. The first time since 2010 Villa moved into sixth place, but not only that, the team were playing with the fluidity and confidence that every Villa fan has been longing to see. It really was pleasing to the eye, and the £20m goalkeeper, Emi Martínez was proving to be as valuable as Ollie Watkins.

The good start of the season was put down to "confidence" according to Jack, speaking to AVTV, "The spine of the team has been really impressive, then up front, Ollie (Watkins), who I can't speak highly enough of, is always willing to learn and wants to improve so much, and I think that's obviously helped us."

By that time, Ross Barkley was proving to be the player most of us thought he could be, and his partnership in midfield with Jack was dynamite. It was reported that Jack pleaded with Barkley during the short summer break to sign on loan for Villa and the fans could see why. They say first impressions count and that was very much true of Ross Barkley, who started his loan spell on fire.

Everyone is aware how the COVID-19 lockdowns affected individual lives, and maybe professional sports people are in a privileged position in that they continued to 'go to work' by and large during most of the national lockdowns. As for Jack, he was no saint as he broke the rules three times. Firstly, he broke the 'stay at home' national coronavirus lockdown rules and was involved in a car accident in March 2020, and in October 2020 he was caught speeding on the M42 on his way to training at Bodymoor Heath, in an attempt not to be late. Both incidents proved costly for Jack, as he was fined and lost his licence for eight months. Then in December 2020, Jack and his Villa teammate, Ross Barkley appeared to break social distancing rules when they were reportedly spotted in a Mayfair restaurant celebrating Barkley's 27th birthday. However, the club took no action on that occasion as it was deemed not serious enough to investigate.

Jack was obviously apologetic and spoke to the Telegraph about the incidents, "As you get older, you learn that you are a hero and role model to younger lads. You need to watch what you are doing. That's not to say that I won't make mistakes, I probably still will. I feel like I have grown up over the years. Hopefully I can carry on doing that. I am a captain of a Premier League club and I just need to take it in my stride. At the moment, I absolutely love my life."

In another interview, this time with the Express & Star, Jack was philosophical about his past and told Matt Maher, "Everything that has happened in my life, I would not change anything. That is the God's honest truth. You know when bad stuff happens in your life and you think: 'I wish that didn't happen'. But looking back on it now, I would want everything to stay the same. I'm a firm believer in everything happening for a reason, and everything that has happened has helped me become the man I am today. I honestly would not change the past."

That's pretty heavy stuff, and respect to Jack for owning up and being honest enough to say that he's only human.

By Christmas, Jack was still on fire. He had created no less than 38 chances from open play alone and 43 in total, more than any player in European footballs' top leagues. According to Dean Smith, he was "performing on another level". He was outperforming the likes of Kevin De Bruyne and Bruno Fernandes. In the game at The Hawthorns on 20th December, Villa won convincingly, 3 – 0, but Jack created eight opportunities, something that no player in the Premier League had achieved in the past five seasons, let alone that season. You could almost hear Dean Smith purring when he spoke to the Telegraph about Jack, "There's more to come from him, definitely. There's still improvements. Sometimes he picks the ball up a little bit too deep. He wants to be involved in the game all the time, but he is on another level at the moment. He's playing wonderful football. At West Brom, it looked like he was playing in the playground with his mates. It was a fantastic performance and, with the levels he's got to, we need to keep pushing him and squeezing even more out of him where he can. He's a joy to watch."

He was playing as an archetypal number 10, floating around the pitch, almost gliding like a ballet dancer on a stage, and he was running at defenders like he always has done. By Christmas, he had been fouled 56 times, 20 more than the nearest, Sadio Mane. Maybe one thing missing from his game, is the ability to score a dozen or more goals, like Lampard or Gerrard did in their day. If he did that, he'd be worth £200m, let alone £100m.

With 2020 coming to an end, it will be seen as the "Year of Jack Grealish' and the time when he finally grabbed the national conscience by the collar and got the attention of the whole country.

Two more defeats followed a draw at Chelsea just after Christmas, ending a run of five games unbeaten, including three victories and four clean sheets. The month of January was a mixed bag for Villa, with three defeats and two wins. Something unusual happened during the home victory against Newcastle. After creating the second goal for Bertrand Traoré in the 42nd minute, Jack was surprisingly substituted late on in the game. Even though the game had been won by then, his disappointment at being subbed broke a run of 42 games playing every minute since October 2019. "I spoke to the manager about that. I was devastated," he told Matt Maher of the Express & Star, "I hadn't come off for 42 games. I was desperate to stay on. I always want to be on the pitch, no matter how tired I am or how tired the manager thinks I am."

As club captain for almost two years, Jack was excited with the new signings the manager and board had brought into the club (both in the summer and in the January transfer window) and spoke to Matt Maher of the Express & Star, "I knew we wouldn't be down there battling relegation. But I would have thought we might be 11th, 12th or 13th, somewhere like that. To be where we are with games in hand is obviously massive. The recruitment over the summer was brilliant and they brought in brilliant players who have all hit the ground running straight away. Hopefully Morgan Sanson (who signed in January from Marseille) can do the same and add that extra bit of bite to midfield. One of the main things you need if you are fighting at the top is squad depth. I feel we have that now."

One of the talking points up to then was how much Jack's game had improved and especially the number of chances he created for others. He told the Peter Crouch Podcast, "One of the things I've been working on this season, and I watch clips with the manager, was my final ball. Last season I created a lot of chances, I think I was third or fourth last year, but I didn't have the assists – I only got six assists. That's what I've tried to do this year. When I get into these areas, a lot of the time I get doubled up, obviously if I'm being doubled up it must mean someone else is free, so I try and set them off. That's what I've worked on the most over the summer and it's paying off now, as I'm on nine assists (as of 5th February 2021) and we're only halfway through the season."

Free-kicks are one part of Jack's game that he has never really developed, even though when he does take one, it usually ends up close to the goal. Jack revealed to the Peter Crouch Podcast that he had been working on his free-kicks and he remembered practicing with his England teammates during one international camp, "The lads were practicing free-kicks after training, and as you can imagine, when you go away with the national team the standard's just so much different to when you're at your club. There were about six or seven of the lads just whipping them in constantly, and I remember the manager saying to me, 'do you not fancy it?' and I said, 'I've never really took them if I'm honest, if anything it's probably my downfall in my game'. Watching the likes of Bruno Fernandes and De Bruyne just getting on them and scoring and getting their stats up, so I thought it's something I'm going to have to start working on." Jack revealed that he and Ross Barkley started working on free-kicks after that England camp in October 2020 and they started staying back after training practicing. I think that shows the perfectionist in Jack, that he was worried about his lack of free-kick taking and wanted to perfect it, if people were going to compare him with the likes of De Bruyne.

The 16th February 2021 signalled a year since Villa Park had fans inside the stadium and it was ironic that, arguably the most talented Villa side in many years had performed in front of no fans (due to the COVID19 restrictions), and that clearly had put a damper on what they had achieved up to that point, as Jack explained to Matt Maher, "There is nothing better than coming to Villa Park when it is packed.

I have told a lot of the lads, Cashy, Ollie (Watkins) and Ross (Barkley): 'Just you wait till you see it full'. At the start of the season, we all hoped by now we would have the fans in, but it wasn't meant to be."

In an interview with the Aston Villa website, Jack explained how different it was playing in front of no fans, "It's been difficult. It's something we're used to now. We're having one of our best seasons in a while. It would have been lovely if the fans had have been here. There are plenty of players playing week in, week out who have never played at Villa Park in front of the fans." The same interview also gave us an insight in what the players did during the first lockdown, "We were sent stuff to do at home, luckily I've got a gym now at my house so I was in there most of the time on the treadmill, bike, doing my own gym work. It weren't too different to what we do here (at the training ground) apart from the actual training side of things."

With the season going well for both Villa and for Jack, the media were talking about him being a candidate for Player of the Year, but on the eve of a tough home game against Leicester City, news came in that Jack had sustained a shin injury during training – it was the news all Villa fans didn't want to hear. After playing in every league game since November 2019, everyone knew how important Jack was to the team. That news was a bitter blow. Dean Smith was apparently furious that the injury had allegedly been leaked, via social media, to Leicester manager, Brendon Rodgers. Reaching him just 24 hours before the game on 21st February gave him time to plan for the game without their Villa talisman. He was ruled out initially for a month, but missing that game meant Jack ended a run of 48 consecutive starts for Villa. At the time, Villa manager Dean Smith gave little away and said it wasn't a long-term injury, "He has had some discomfort in training this week,' Smith informed Sky Sports, "At the top of the week, we were determined he wasn't proper to play." Pressed for how lengthy he thought Jack would be out for, Smith added, "We do not consider it is a long-term injury. We're simply going to evaluate him as he goes. I've no concept [how long he'll be out for]. I'm hopeful. I'm all the time an optimist."

After that game against Leicester, which ended in a Villa defeat, manager Dean Smith explained just how important his captain is to the team, he added: "His value just goes up and up. I won't stop talking about him because he is genuine quality. He takes two or three players out the game. It's just genuine quality and without him today they have been a shadow of the team we have seen this season."

Dean Smith quickly dismissed fears that it was a reoccurrence of an old shin injury he suffered two seasons previously but couldn't give any more details about it or when Jack would be available again. The only thing Smith could say was that his team would be without Jack for a while.

The only bit of comfort Villa fans could take from the injury blow to Jack was that Smith had built a competitive top-flight team – even if Jack has played such a vital role in much of the good things Villa had done up until then. It wasn't much comfort, but it was all that was on offer.

So, how would Villa cope without the midfield general? His absence no doubt reflected in a drop off in form or at least performance levels, though there was a hope that Smith could have galvanised his squad to maintain a healthy points' haul during the period Jack was out; however, by and large, that wasn't the case. There was no doubt that the high intensity the team play at with him in the side simply wasn't there without him. It certainly was a bump in the road that Smith needed to address in their pursuit of a European place, which was quite possible until the point Jack got injured. There was a real opportunity to unite the dressing room and prove the squad's worth, and to try and replace the quality and value that Jack brings to the table. For Smith, he had to shuffle the pack, find a new captain and think of a different way to play.

The frustrating thing for Villa fans during the period Jack was injured was the lack of information coming out of Villa Park, and what information there was, seemed confusing. Firstly, we were told Jack was complaining of lower leg pain in the build-up to the Leicester game, but that subsequently turned out to be 'shin splints'. The Birmingham Mail reported on 2nd March that he may have been fit to face Wolves on 6th March. Even the most optimistic fan must have thought that was over-ambitious to say the least. However, Dean Smith reported shortly afterwards, "Jack will still be out for this game. He's still got pain on a particular movement he's got. He's working with the doctor and the rehab staff every day. It's frustrating because he's a top player and we're a better team for having him in it."

By the Newcastle game on 12th March, Dean Smith said, "Jack's been making really good progress but, unfortunately, he won't make Newcastle," confirming Jack would miss his fifth match on the spin, "He has been ill this week so he's been off for a couple of days as well, but we're hopeful for the Tottenham game now, that's for sure."

After the Spurs home defeat and before the Fulham game on 4th April, things were still not looking good. Dean Smith explained that even though Jack was keen to play the medical people had taken a more cautious approach, "He had trained in the week but he had some discomfort in training yesterday. He was all for playing but had discomfort and we have to be cautious. We'll see how it goes."

While Jack had been out, the team had struggled. In the six games that he had missed, Villa had only won once; they had lost three games and drew twice. The club fell to 11th place in the league before the fixture against Fulham. During that period, they also managed only three goals without him.

Those figures proved Jack's importance to Villa cannot be understated. His very presence was integral to Dean Smith's side on and off the pitch.

The Villa skipper took to Instagram early in April and uploaded a snap of him working with strength and conditioning coach Oli Stevenson at Bodymoor Heath. The snap set off the Villa fans, who immediately thought it was a sign that Jack was about to return to training. Jack appeared to be on the spinning machines and attached his picture with the caption, **'we working'.** He also took to Twitter on 9th April with a picture of him on a bike with the caption:
"Missing it so bad! Doing everything to be back fitter and stronger than ever."

As time went by and there was still no information about the injury and no indication how serious it was, until the 9th April, when Dean Smith admitted to the media that Jack was expected to be out for another two weeks at least, after suffering a setback in his attempt to get back training. He told the press conference before the away trip to Anfield, "He's trained this week and was looking good, but had some discomfort yesterday, so pulled out after 10 minutes in training, so we have to err on the side of caution as we must do with these injuries." He also added that he had been rushed back "a little bit too quickly." However, he did also add, "Myself and Jack were quite optimistic to get him back a bit sooner than he probably should and he's had a setback that will probably put him back a couple of weeks." With that setback in the planned recovery programme, it also meant he missed England's trio of World Cup qualifiers and would be out until the end of April, at least.

It was a bitter blow for Jack, for Villa, and for England, "He was really good in training, but he couldn't tolerate the loading. It's a loading injury and we have to de-load him over the next few weeks and get him back from there. However, despite the setback, Smith declared he would be available for the Euros in France, "He's proved himself already but the one thing for certain is he will be back before the end of the season, and then Gareth has to make a decision whether he thinks he's right for that. He has played 20-odd games this season, so everybody has a good idea of what his form is and what he's about."

Dean Smith then provided a further update to his skipper's injury during the Manchester City pre-match press conference on 20th April by saying Jack was "pencilled in for Everton on May 1" and also stressed, "He's pain free but, as I said a few weeks ago, we're not going to rush him back." Jack was spotted in the stands by the TV cameras during the Manchester City game talking to Gareth Southgate; I wonder what was said? I would imagine they discussed Jack's injury; Southgate must have been making regular checks on his fitness so to keep in his thoughts for the Euros in the summer.

The Sun newspaper claimed back in April that Jack may not play again until May at least, but Villa boss Smith explained the situation in further detail ahead of the drawn game against West Bromwich Albion on 25th April. Smith confirmed that Jack was set to undergo another scan on his shin. However, some positive news was revealed as his hopes of making England's Euro 2020 squad were given a boost because the squad sizes had been increased from 23 to 26, so that meant Jack would stand a better chance of being picked for the Euros.

Three days later, Dean Smith suggested in the pre-West Bromwich Albion press conference that Jack wouldn't be fit for the Everton game after all and was going to have another scan to try and clear up if he's fit to start training. Smith said he would probably miss the Everton and Manchester United games and pencilled in Crystal Palace as the next target.

By the end of April, Dean Smith still remained hopeful that his star man would be returning to the training ground before too long, but it was too soon to feature at Everton at Goodison on 1st May. By then, he'd been out for 70 days and had missed 10 games. Smith again reaffirmed to the Birmingham Mail that Jack would be back before the end of the season and would be fit for the Euros in June. The next target was for Jack to return to training ahead of the home game with Manchester United, "He's working on his own at the moment. As I say, it's going to be a gradual loading. It's a loading stress injury so we can't rush him. I think because of the last time (aggravating it before Fulham) he broke down a bit so we're a little tentative so will probably want to take a different approach to last time. I expect him to be training with us next week."

It was later confirmed by Smith that the scan came back with positive results, and he hoped Jack would return to full training ahead of the home game against Manchester United on 9th May.

The Duke of Cambridge, Prince William then visited Bodymoor Heath on 4th May to open the new state-of-the-art high-performance centre and he spoke to Jack about his injury, and his reply was as vague as Dean Smith's previous forecasts had been, "I haven't actually got a date yet but I'm going to London on Thursday (for a scan). I'm hoping a week or 10 days." A day or so later, Jack returned to training but was ruled out of the home game against Manchester United on 9th May, but Dean Smith claimed he could be back for the re-arranged home fixture against Everton on the 13th May.

By that time, Jack's 12-game absence saw Villa slip from Europa

League contenders to battling to stay in the top half whilst finding themselves eight points off the top six. Villa fans must have wondered how good the season would have been if Jack hadn't have missed so many games from the end of February. They say that statistics don't lie, and that seems clear enough when you analyse Villa's performance and results without Jack in the side. From the time he got injured in training just before the Leicester game on 21st February 2021, he'd scored six goals and had 10 assists. In the 12 games he missed Villa had gone from 8th in the Premier League with 35 points and pushing for a place in Europe, to 11th and 48 points:

Won 3, Lost 6, Drawn 3

The stats only added more weight to the theory that Villa were over-reliant on Jack, but football is a team game and that shouldn't be the case, but Jack is a special talent and any team would miss a player who'd contributed to 16 goals by the middle of the season. Is Villa a 'one-man team'? Maybe? Watching Villa without their maestro is like watching a horse without a jockey. There was a lack of invention or magic in the final third of the pitch; Jack provides that spark that can't easily be replaced.

It is remarkable to think that Jack still ranked top of Europe's top five leagues for carries into the penalty box with a total of 76, ahead of Kylian Mbappe in second on 66 and Marcus Rashford in third on 61. That is quite an astounding stat considering his lack of game time. In addition to getting the ball to valuable areas, Jack also showcased an ability to present his teammates with opportunities to shoot at goal, averaging 3.4 key passes per 90 in the Premier League, and that put him ahead of Kevin De Bruyne and Bruno Fernandes.

During a heavy run of games towards the end of the shortened season, Dean Smith admitted his skipper would be back in some capacity for the mid-week, re-arranged fixture against Everton, after a week of full training under his belt. That assumption turned out to be true, as Jack was named as a substitute. He wasn't close to starting games, with Smith saying to the pre-Everton press conference, "Is he ready to start games? No, but if he feels pain-free then he's ready to be a part of the squad."

After so much speculation from the media about his fitness and coyness from Dean Smith, Jack finally took to the field for the first time in 12 games with 18 minutes to go in the goalless draw against Everton, replacing Bertrand Traore. He then managed another 26 minutes in the defeat at Crystal Palace.

With a total of 44 minutes on the pitch in the last 14 games, Jack was seen as ready to start in the away fixture at Tottenham, and what a game it turned out to be. With Spurs needing to win to move into the Europa League places, Villa dented their chances after coming back from being a goal down within 10 minutes and leading at half-time. The score remained 2 – 1 and Jack lasted 73 minutes before being replaced by Douglas Luiz. It was a superb performance and Villa's first win against Spurs for six years. The game also saw the return of fans into stadiums, with 10,000 home fans being allowed into the new Tottenham Hotspur Stadium.

It was remarkable to think that Villa Park saw the return of fans for the first time in 462 days, since Villa's 3 – 2 defeat to Spurs on 16th February 2020. Dean Smith expected Jack to start again against Chelsea for the final game of the season, "He's getting up to full fitness, he showed a real confidence in his performance at Tottenham and hopefully we will see more of that on Sunday."

The season finished on a high with a hard-earned 2 – 1 win against Chelsea in front of 10,000 passionate Villa fans.

So, with the season at a close, Dean Smith told the pre-Chelsea press conference he was pleased at the 11th place finish, "It pleases me, but it doesn't surprise me. The performances have been there – there has been an inconsistency since our COVID break, we know that. To finish 11th, which is where we will finish now, is an improvement of six places and that's with only bringing five players in. I'm very pleased, in general, with how the players have performed and improved. That will continue." Talking about Jack in general, Smith added, "That's the positive outlook for me. We've had an injury to Jack this season where we lost him for 13 games, and that's been pivotal to where we've finished in the league."

Rounding up the season, Smith also spoke to the Express & Star and said he was disappointed with the poor final third of the season, "It is very rare a team goes from staying up on the last day of the season to challenging for Champions League places. While our ambitions are still to be there and we have been disappointed with the last 16 to 17 games, we certainly note that progression." Smith is aware Villa's early-season promise saw expectations rise enormously, especially amongst the fans, but he added: "That is something I am not looking to dampen. Those ambitions are our ambitions. We knew it would be tough to compete for Europe this season but I think we have been up and around there probably until the last five or six games, which shows a massive progression. We are disappointed we have dropped off but that has coincided with Jack coming out of the team and he has been our biggest chance creator in the last few years. You are always looking to get momentum. The one thing I can't criticise my players for is their attitude and their effort this season."

While it would be difficult to speculate about Villa's position in the table if Jack had remained fit throughout, it is reasonable to suggest that a finish inside the top half would have been realistic, given the position they were in before his injury. His level up until his setback was remarkable, with Villa developing a tendency to lean on his qualities as a means of securing positive results.

If you look at the season in terms of numbers and Jack's influence on games, it was evident Jack made an enormous contribution on the pitch which was paramount to Villa's success:

	With Jack	Without Jack
Games:	26	12
Win %:	50	25
Goals for:	42	13
Goals Against:	29	17
Points Per Game:	1.7	1.0

Then, if you look at his personal stats for the 2020 – 2021 season, he was up there with his numbers, even though he missed a third of the season:

Goals:	6
Assists:	10
Fouls won:	110
Fouls won per game:	4.53 (1st in the Premier League)
Assists per game:	0.41 (2nd in the Premier League)
Chances created per game:	3.31 (2nd in the Premier League)

****

All through the season there was loose talk of where Jack would be, come the summer of 2021 – if anywhere other than Villa Park. The media frenzy never stopped and they were convinced he would move on, to a Champions League club. Manchester United and Manchester City were the two clubs talked about the most. However, at the time it was all hypothetical and whether it affected Jack was unknown; certainly, it didn't affect him on the pitch. Jack had never been more central to the clubs' present and future, as he was during the period he was injured. Jack Grealish is the embodiment of their hunger and ambition and the club knew they needed to match that if they wanted to keep hold of their star man.

Villa seemed like a club on the up, with owners who weren't frightened to splash the cash; they started the 2020 – 2021 season with a bang after their desire to improve the playing squad. They found themselves in a symbiotic dynamic where they needed to attract better players to help persuade Jack to stay and keeping him at the club will be a key draw for any new player thinking of joining.

Villa were in no rush to sell Jack at the beginning of the 2020 – 2021 season, nor were they at the end of it. Dean Smith was all too aware of the conundrum he was faced throughout the season and at the end of it. Speaking to Stadium Astro during the season, he said, "If we don't keep progressing and become a club that's challenging in Europe, then we probably won't meet Jack's ambitions and there will be a time when Jack looks elsewhere."

That comment suggested the club would do anything to help keep Jack at the club, and that included buying quality players who improved the team, not just the squad. Jack needs to be around quality players, so whether Villa can get to a level befitting of their standout player, or at least in a quick enough timescale, remains to be seen but, in the meantime, his upward trajectory certainly bodes well for club and country. The club will want to make up that gap during the 2021 – 2022 season, with Smith, Purslow and sporting director Johan Lange tasked with the finding players to complement their star asset, players who can compete with the very best as Villa will look to bolster their squad once again, "We know we have an exceptional talent on our hands," Smith told the Birmingham Mail, when discussing the need to build a team around Jack, a player who's watched his England teammates Mason Mount and Phil Foden rip it up in the Champions League during the 2020 – 2021 season. Especially Foden, who has taken advantage of the absence of Jack during the tail end of the season and helped Manchester City get to the Champions' League Final. Smith continued, "We make sure we are looking to improve as a squad next season. We bought in 13 new faces in 2019; five this season (2020 – 2021) and we have to add to that squad to keep improving. That's what you have to do to be a force in the Premier League. Next year will be our third season in the Premier League, you are playing catch up with the bigger clubs. The finances they have had has enabled them to be stronger. We have been planning for this window since the last window closed and probably before that. We have our plans and they will continue to evolve."

During the middle of May 2021, with the season drawing to a close, it was interesting to watch Jack's agent, Jonathan Barnett, who incidentally is the agent to Gareth Bale and Ben Chilwell, being interviewed by Sky News. He admitted in the interview that Jack could stay at Villa for the following season, and beyond. That statement would have made Villa fans happy and was contrary to the endless rumours about Jack's future during the season, and even for the preceding two seasons. Some rumours were seen as pure speculation, some ridiculous and some entirely plausible, but his agent played them down. Even though he himself seemed to have an obsession, getting Jack to sign for Arsenal.

During the interview, Barnett revealed how Jack was attracting strong interest from Europe's big-hitters but said "he could stay" at Aston Villa. He also played down interest from Manchester United, who had been rumoured to have been admirers. Barnett, meanwhile, said Jack would sit down with Villa once more during the summer to plan ahead for next season with Dean Smith targeting European qualification in 2022, "The truth is we don't know what will happen. There are many clubs interested and I wouldn't put Manchester United at the top of that list. He could stay as well so it's a conversation the club, Aston Villa, will have with Jack and ourselves then we'll see where we go." Barnett also detailed what Villa fans already knew, that Jack loves being at Villa, while talking up his prospects of lighting it up for England at the upcoming Euros, "At the moment he is a Villa player and he has no thoughts about anything else. He could be a big star in the summer, he maybe should have been playing a little bit earlier for England. It is unfortunate that he has got this injury at the moment but that will be fine. The only hope is, he is given a chance and he will be great."

With Jack part of the England Euro 2020 squad, there were constant rumours all summer about Jack. All of the top six clubs would want to sign Jack, but it would be very difficult due to the fact he had a long-term contract with Villa, said to be 4 years left on it. In fact, the ambitious Villa owners were speaking to his agent about offering Jack an improved contract, said to be worth around £150,000 a week.

The message from the Villa camp was clear – they did not want to sell Jack Grealish at any cost.

Manchester City seemed to be the club who were interested in signing him all summer long, but by the semi-finals of Euro 2020, Villa had received no approach from anyone, no offer or no official interest. In fact, Manchester City's priority for the summer was to buy a striker, with Harry Kane high up on their list. Therefore, it appeared unlikely that they would sign a striker costing around £100m and Jack Grealish, who would surely cost a similar amount. Manchester City would only fund those deals by selling players.

The other factor is, did Aston Villa want to sell Jack? The answer to that was a resounding "no". It was obvious that Villa were building around Jack, but in all transfer sagas, it's always interesting to understand who holds the power with certain players, and in this case, the power was with Villa.

Chapter 8

ENGLAND V IRELAND

*Jack was eligible to represent either England or the Republic
of Ireland; he was capped by Ireland up to under-21 level before
confirming his decision to play for England in September 2015.*

Although Jack was born in the leafy suburb of Solihull,
West Midlands, he is of Irish descent through his maternal
grandmother, from County Dublin. His paternal grandfather was
from Gort in County Galway and his paternal grandmother from
Sneem, County Kerry.

Jack had entered a sporting world that required intense dedication,
mental toughness and smart decision-making. Being part of the
Aston Villa football academy for seven years, he was still heavily
influenced by his heritage and Irish background and started
playing Gaelic football for John Mitchel's Hurling and Camogie
Club of Warwickshire GAA in Dorridge, Solihull. Apparently he was
fairly good at it too, playing for Warwickshire GAA at Croke Park
(Ireland's equivalent of Wembley) in 2009 All-Ireland Senior Football
Championship quarter-final between Dublin and Kerry.

Jack had described Gaelic football as "quite technical and rough"
and he used to get whacked all the time, which he said helped him
as a Premier League player. Jack loved playing the sport and when
he was at St Peter's Roman Catholic School in Solihull, his love of
the Gaelic game was matched by the school, who really pushed it. It
was a summer sport in Ireland so when the football season ended,
young Jack didn't take to cricket, he'd prefer to play Gaelic football.
According to Jack's father, Kevin, speaking to the Birmingham Mail,
the Irish sport toughened his son up and made 'proper' football

far easier, "He'd run the show playing Gaelic. It really helped him because he was knocked from pillar to post. It's brutal compared to soccer. Jack is good with his feet but he can pick the ball up as well and he'd flick it around everyone! I told Gordon Cowans this once. He asked why Jack was so good at expecting tackles it was the GAA. It really built up his upper body, players would bounce off him. It's probably why he so strong today. He had to stop playing though, they'd just be stamping on his fingers and it became all too much. We had Nike knocking at the door at this point as well who wanted to sponsor him."

Indeed, Jack had to stop playing Gaelic football, given the fact that the older you get, the rougher the game gets; in fact, the coaches at Villa told him to stop as he was becoming quite a decent footballer and they didn't want him injured playing another sport.

The tug-of-war between the Ireland FA and the England FA began in 2010, when Jack, aged 14, was offered a trial by England, but he bizarrely missed out on playing in the Victory Shield after jumping out of bed too quickly in the team hotel, fainting and crashing to the bathroom floor, "I was just a young lad, going to meet up with all the best players from England, and it was a big difference from what I was used to. When I got there, I woke up in the middle of the night and went to go to the toilet. My room-mate, who was Diego Poyet (Gus Poyet's son) heard a bang and then I just woke up in the bathroom. I had obviously collapsed. I didn't want to go home the following day, but England said they thought it was best that I did."

Although Jack was desperate to get another chance with England, the Republic of Ireland also asked him join their ranks too, and he accepted. He was in demand even at an early age. Scout, Mark O'Toole had alerted Ireland to Jack's heritage after spotting him playing in the Nike Premier Cup. Jack said, "From then on, I went to play for Ireland through the youth levels and I carried on with them because of how much I enjoyed it." Some of his Villa academy mates, including Samir Carruthers and Mickey Drennan were all playing for Ireland at the time and they loved the set up, but Jack didn't enjoy staying away on international duty. Both of his mates' careers took off in different directions, and so did Jack's.

The difference between Jack and his other two Villa academy mates was that he felt more English than Irish; indeed, he was fully English, even though he had the choice between two countries for his international football career, if that decision had to be made. Jack went on to represent Ireland at Under-17, Under-18 and Under-21 level a total of 19 times, but he was always undecided who he'd rather play for if he ever got called up to the full international squad, be it Ireland or England.

For Jack, it would be an important decision to make, because of the international rules, which state if a player plays for full-international, he can't represent another nation, unlike the rules at Under-21 level and below.

According to the regulations governing the application of the FIFA statutes:

"If a player has more than one nationality, or if a player acquires a new nationality, or if a player is eligible to play for several representative teams due to nationality, he may, only once, request to change the Association for which he is eligible to play international matches to the Association of another country of which he holds nationality."

In 2012, former England Under-17 coach, John Peacock said, "Myself and Under-16 head coach, Kenny Swain had several discussions with him (Jack) about switching back, but he was undecided." Another invitation to join the England Under-17 was turned down. This was the encouragement that the FAI wanted and at that stage, Jack was apparently veering towards Ireland; however, doubts were cast as he was omitted from the Irish Under-21 squad in October 2012.

That omission from the Irish squad prompted another approach from England, and Ireland Under-21 coach Noel King revealed in May 2013 that Jack was eying another attempt to play for England. The FAI refused to wilt, having already had a similar situation in Michael Keane, who later went on to play for England. However, King acted swiftly and made Jack one of the youngest ever player to represent Ireland Under-21s, at the age of 17, when he came on as a substitute against the Faroe Islands. He earned his first full start against Germany and scored his first goal against the Faroe Islands in November 2013.

It wasn't until the summer of 2014 that the dilemma reached boiling point when Jack pulled out of an Irish Under-21 squad preparing for a game against Norway in favour of playing for Villa in a friendly. That decision effectively distanced himself from ever playing for Ireland's senior team. Villa's manager back then, Paul Lambert, described Jack as being "torn" and said, "I didn't want him to make the wrong decision. You have to be comfortable playing for an international side."

By March 2015, with Tim Sherwood now in the Villa hotseat, Jack was seemingly still confused and undecided. Jack clearly considered it a sufficiently important honour to have his entire family present when he collected the FAI Under-21 player of the year award. At the awards, Jack said he had taken a year out of international football to concentrate on playing club football but promised he would play for Ireland soon. To add to the mixed messages, there was always that doubt in the Irish FAI that he was 'too English' and would eventually pick the Three Lions.

Tim Sherwood did his best to guide Jack with his "follow your heart" speech in the media, "Don't chose Ireland just because you think you'll get into the team quicker." Two months later he turned down another approach from Ireland, this time for friendlies against England and a Euro qualifier against Scotland.

Ever since Jack was seen as 'the next best thing...' there was a long-running battle going on in footballing circles, whether Jack would choose Ireland or England, with both nations desperate for his services. That battle intensified after the FA Cup semi-final between Aston Villa and Liverpool in April 2015 when Jack played out of his skin and helped his side make it through to the Final and subsequently had a major impact in Villa's escape from relegation. It was understood that the Ireland manager tried to entice Jack into playing for his side before the semi-final, but he was warned off by his father.

In May 2015, Roy Hodgson seemed to be getting a bit agitated waiting for Jack to make up his mind by saying, "If he doesn't want to play or he has doubts, then don't play. We are doing him a favour by picking him – not him doing us a favour by turning up."

The war of words between Roy Hodgson and Martin O'Neill continued to spill over when the Irish manager said on talkSPORT Radio, "What I've said to him is that he's a fairly decent chance, a better chance, of getting into our team than he would have of getting into England in the foreseeable future. There's wee things we think that we might be able to help along the way." During the same press conference, O'Neill's assistant, Roy Keane chipped in, "He's a really nice kid. People have been too hard on him lately, and if he comes and plays for us, brilliant. But if he goes and plays for England, then you have got to respect the decision. Whether you like it or not is irrelevant. You have got to accept it."

Jack apparently turned down Martin O'Neill's offer of making his senior debut in the friendly against England of all teams on 7th June 2015 at the Aviva Stadium. O'Neill tried a second time, asking him to join up for the squad to take on Scotland in a Euro 2016 qualifier. Again, Jack turned down the offer, "We appreciated the call from Martin yesterday but there was no way Jack was going to accept," said Kevin Grealish to the Irish Times, "I reiterated to Martin what we had told the Ireland U-21 manager (Noel King). Jack opted to take the year out to concentrate on Aston Villa and that decision has proved to be correct one based upon how he's doing lately."

It also transpired that if Jack had been approached by Roy Hodgson, he would have received the same answer. In fact, Roy Hodgson was thinking of playing Jack, if he had chosen England by that date, against Ireland at the Aviva Stadium; however, Hodgson said, "it would have been inflammatory at the last minute if he chose us and played." It had been Hodgson's intention to include Jack in two dead-rubber qualifiers against Estonia and Lithuania or if he hadn't decided by then, include him in a series of friendlies leading up to the Euro Finals in France.

The summer of 2015 was no time to make rash decisions that would rule his future playing career. Jack was focused on helping Villa escape relegation and of course, wanted to play in the FA Cup Final on 30th May. If Villa had nothing to play for, then either Martin O'Neill or Roy Hodgson would have got their man. "Nothing can act as a distraction to keeping his place. Had Jack taken up Martin's offer, the level of attention and pressure on him at this late stage of the season would have been enormous. Jack will complete the club season, hopefully with an FA Cup winners' medal, before taking a break. After that, we'll look at the international situation," Tim Sherwood said to the media.

Tim Sherwood wasn't going to influence Jack which way he should lean, even though he must have wished he'd choose England, "He hasn't told me. I can't tell him. In his heart of hearts, he has to decide whether he is English or Irish. He has to decide."

Jack had to make the right decision for him - the right footballing decision, that is. To make a declaration for England would be a decision to back himself 100%, to announce that he believed in himself that he was among the very best of English footballers. It would have been massive decision. To declare to play for a country with a semi-professional league and, despite a few summers of fun in major competitions had a generally patchy record in the international game, that would also be a huge call.

There was a belief amongst the Irish at the time that if Jack decided to wear the green of Ireland at senior level, it was because he wanted to play for Ireland above all else; not because England didn't choose him but because he didn't choose England.

That decision was reportedly made early in September 2015, when he declared his intention to play for England, but this was rejected by his father, his father told reporters Jack hadn't played much football that season, due to multiple injuries and lack of game time. Although England had already qualified, and with only a couple of qualifying games for the Euro 2016 approaching, England manager Roy Hodgson was still waiting for Jack's decision, just like everyone else. In fact, Roy Hodgson's patience had apparently worn thin, "I'm not 100% certain of what he is waiting for. I would like him to come out and say. 'I've thought about it, I've got the two possibilities and I'm opting for England' and then he will be available for selection." To that comment, Martin O'Neill responded in a press conference by saying, "Well, that's encouraging, it's encouraging anyway. Roy is not going to hang around, so well-done Roy, putting the pressure on."

It seemed both international managers were trying to entice Jack using the media, both using different tactics.

Jack vowed to tell the England manager well before the Euros so he could plan for the tournament; he also told Ireland manager, Martin O'Neil that he would decide either way in time for preparations for the last pair of those qualifying games. He and his father sat down with both managers to discuss Jack's options and both wanted to fast-track him into their squads in time.

As it transpired Martin O'Neill and Roy Keane had been looking at Jack since he was on loan at Notts County (2013 - 2014), "He was playing for Ireland's Under-21s and physically, he was nowhere near as strong as he is now, but there were definitely signs he could be a really good player. He's clever, he is very good at shielding the ball with his body and he has a good eye for an inside pass. He would have given us something we so obviously lacked in the final third and it was disappointing for us at the time. He had qualities as a player we did not have in abundance in the squad."

By the 28th September 2015, the 'Jack Grealish Saga' was over. Whilst he hadn't played much for Villa in the Premier League, Jack was a still highly regarded by England manager, Roy Hodgson and went all-out to get his man, "It was not an easy decision as Ireland has a special place with me through my family," Jack told the BBC, "But I have decided to represent the country of my birth." Jack subsequently talked about the decision he had to make, to choose between Ireland or England, "As I got older, I realised I am English, my family are English and in the future that's what I want to do."

The decision Jack had made showed a lot of self-confidence and that he was prepared to stick it out and wait his turn. So many players of lesser ability with duel nationalities have opted for the 'easier' option, to play for 'the other country' rather than England, most notably Wilfred Zaha who chose to play for the Ivory Coast instead of fighting for a place in the England set-up, even though he'd played for the Under-19s, Under-21s and even got two senior caps (in friendlies).

Whether or not Martin O'Neill and Roy Keane thought they had any chance of persuading Jack to play for Ireland only they know that. As it transpired the Irish party made it clear they wanted Jack but were also under no illusion that his upbringing, and indeed his father's upbringing was in Birmingham, "The thing that struck us both was that not only was Jack born and raised in Birmingham, but his dad was also a Brummie too. Jack is English. Although he had enjoyed playing for Ireland, when we spoke to him, we quickly realised that was how he saw himself. We hoped he would choose to play for Ireland, but we understood it. The association with Ireland was through his grandparents, not even his father. It might have been different if he had been born in Birmingham and moved to Dublin at some stage as a child, but he had a choice to make. It was frustrating at the time but in those conversations, it was also clear that commercially, there would be a bigger boost for him if he could make it with England." Although O'Neill had no resentment towards Jack or the decision he took, he made it clear that Jack would have been a shoo-in to play for him in the Euro 2016 and he would have helped Ireland qualify for the World Cup in Russia (in 2018).

It was quite clear, reading Martin O'Neill's comments in September 2020 that he sensed Jack would have played many times and would have been a huge superstar for Ireland. Had he have chosen that path five years ago, which sounded like a quip at Jack's decision-making. O'Neill must also be wondering where he is likely to find a player like Jack again, or one with that ability, given the situation over Declan Rice, who had actually played for Ireland three times before changing his allegiance to England.

So, Jack was about to embark on, what he hoped would be a long and fruitful international career. By choosing England, he was guaranteed an opportunity to stake a claim for the Euro 2016 squad and Roy Hodgson was absolutely delighted. His announcement was just in time to be available to play in the Euro 2016 qualifies against Estonia and Lithuania in October 2015; however, the English FA needed to work quickly in order to register him with FIFA.

Although the English camp were pleased at capturing Jack's services, not everyone was happy that he'd chosen his country of birth, as Jack was the subject of a torrent of abuse – and not just from supporters. He was targeted by sportswear companies as well.

Jack admitted to an Irish American sports magazine, Balls.ie that he "didn't expect so much abuse from Ireland fans." Some speculation was going around that his agent at the time had made the decision for him, but that was refuted by Jack himself, "It was a big decision and wasn't easy for me. I thought about it for a long time, spoke with my family and my agent, but in the end it came from me. For my career I think if I fulfil my ability I can play for England in years to come." He also spoke to Oisin McQueirns of Pundit Arena about his decision, "Since I was a kid, I've felt like I'm English. My family are English, it was just my grandparents who are Irish and when I was a young kid I was playing for Ireland because that's what felt right. It felt fun, if anything."

Although Jack's grandparents were Irish, his famous great-great grandfather, Billy Garraty, who played for Aston Villa in the 1905 FA Cup Final, was in fact English, born in Birmingham (in 1878), so in a way, Jack's 'Englishness' wasn't just because of his own place of birth.

Jack had made it clear he wanted to play international football for England, but he still had a job breaking into the full squad. By April 2017, he was still playing for the Under-21s and the Head Coach, Aidy Boothroyd dropped him from the squad for turning up late to a scheduled team meeting, just before an important game against Denmark. Team discipline and togetherness had become part and parcel of the genre of the England set-up at all levels, with every player having to abide by the rules, and that included Jack.

Clearly, Jack had the ability to play for the full England team, and had shown it in the seven Under-21 appearances, but it looked like he faced a waiting game to step up into Gareth Southgate's plans.

Chapter 9

SHINS

Just why does Jack wear his socks round his ankles?

Jack Grealish is the epitome of a modern-day footballing superstar - sublime skills, lashings of boldness and imagination, exceptional ability, power and stamina, the ability to take on defenders at pace. Add to that list, the slicked back hair, socks at half-mast revealing a pair of shinpads the size of postage stamps. Jack is the ultimate showstopper and he stands out from the crowd.

So, what's with the rolled down socks and the lack of 'proper' shinpads during matches? Is it just a story about another footballer's superstition?

Apparently, it all started at primary school. Jack was never a flamboyant player when he was young according to his former head teacher, but now his style of play is regarded as 'individual' - and he has the reputation of going down too easily. So, why doesn't he wear 'proper' shinpads?

When 99% of players protect their prized assets (their shins) Jack goes onto the football field with his socks rolled down. Some people have been tricked into thinking that the skilful playmaker doesn't wear shinpads – but he does. In fact, he wears what are called junior 'shinnies', somewhere between age 5 and 7. One reason why he chooses to wear the minuscule protectors is that he finds the shin pads that are larger and go further up his legs are too restrictive. However, another reason behind his trademark look is down to an accidental shrinking incident, "Obviously your socks are supposed to go above your calves," Jack was quoted as saying in 2015. He continued, "But one year when I was here, the socks shrunk in the wash. So, they wouldn't go higher. That season, I ended up playing really well. So, it became a superstitious thing for me. I thought, 'I'm going to keep doing this because I've done well.' It's become something of a trademark for me." Although referees are obliged to make sure players are safe on the pitch, they have no power over what size shinpads the players chose. Jack also suggested, "A few referees have tried telling me but I've got to keep it like that."

There's also another reason behind the practice – the size of Jack's calves. According to Jack, "A lot of socks are so tight around my calves that they give me cramp. I try to have them down underneath my calves." The size and shape of his claves have become a talking point during live Villa games recently, but Jack insists he hasn't ever worked on them and said, "my Grandad had big calves, so has my mum, so it's just a thing that runs in my family."

Paul Lambert, when he was managing Jack at Villa apparently had no problem with the way he wore his low-cut socks and his junior shin-pads but was concerned he wasn't protected enough from flying tackles; it was more about if Jack was comfortable with the way he wore his socks then it was OK with Lambert.

According to the former Villa academy director, Bryan Jones, Jack used to "drive Tony McAndrew (former Aston Villa Youth Team coach) mad" when he trained with his socks down to his ankles and threatened to pull him off if he didn't pull his socks up. Whether Jack actually pulled his socks up is unknown, but Jack is his own man and you can make up your own assumptions on that score. Having said that, if his manager or coach is comfortable in allowing his players to play without proper shin pads and with their socks rolled down, then what's the problem - as long as the player is comfortable and that certainly seems the case with Jack. I suppose playing devils' advocate, if you're a youth team player you should do as you're told, but as soon as that person becomes a senior pro, I suppose he can do as he likes, and that sums it up about Jack, his socks and his shin pads – or lack of them.

From an outsider's viewpoint, wearing his socks the way he does and the use of junior shinpads is more evidence that Jack has a character and is a 'character'; we don't want robots on the pitch, I believe there are too many robotic players these days, who are just going through the motions, playing the way they've been told and dressing the way they have been asked to. A lot of the players are all much of a muchness and quite frankly, are boring to watch; maybe some fans expect 'robots' to turn up every week? Those characters from yesteryear are sadly disappearing from the game, so for me, the more Jack Grealish's there are, the better for the modern game.

From watching Jack at close quarters for the many years now, I get the distinct impression he really loves playing, loves winning and really wants to improve himself. That can't be said for some modern-day footballers. Personally, I like players who have 'something' about them; players who have a bit of flair and can express themselves on the pitch. Jack stands out for me because he has his socks rolled down and doesn't use shin pads – and don't forget his Alice bands - now, that alone makes him stand out. He also has a special quality and a certain cheekiness about him and the way he plays the game as well which makes him stand out above the rest. Going back in time, George Best was a prime example. You never saw him wear his shirt tucked in, well maybe occasionally, but most of time he'd take the field with his shirt hanging out. Much the same with Jack, not that I'm comparing him to the great George Best, but both players had / have that 'something' about them that makes them stand out from the rest of the crowd; I guess the word is 'individualism'.

Talking about George Best, there were rumours that Jack wore his socks so low because he'd watched old footage of the Manchester United great, who also ghosted past defenders with ease, and with his socks around his ankles, much the same as Jack does. However, Jack apparently quashed that idea, "A lot of people say that it's because of George Best. While I love him and admire so much what he did, that isn't the reason. It's a superstition that I've done all my life and I'm going to keep it that way."

Football fans love to see 'characters' or 'individuals' in the game; there are a lack of them that's for sure. Jack Grealish certainly is an 'individual' footballer of the modern era. You can't teach that, and there's no reason for coaches to teach him to play any other way or dress any other way, not that there has been any evidence of that so far in his career. It seems that if Jack wants to roll down his socks and wear junior shinnies, then Jack will do that and no manager or referee will stop him. I like that in him, so good on Jack for keeping up his superstitions and what makes him feel comfortable.

Even his former Villa manager, Tim Sherwood didn't mind Jack wearing his socks down to his ankles either. Going back to the 2015 FA Cup semi-final against Liverpool at Wembley, probably the day Jack Grealish emerged to the world football stage, the 19-year-old was seen with his now trademark rolled down socks, unafraid to taking ferocious kicks from the Liverpool players. "It's just his style," Tim said, "If he performs how I think he can, he can dress how he wants. It's not a fashion show. He is good and perhaps he knows he's good. You know what he said to me when I told him he was playing? He just said: 'Bout time!'"

One thing that Jack wouldn't have celebrated at the end of Villa's first back in the Premier League, was becoming the most fouled player in any season since the Premier League started; he was clearly the most fouled player in the three seasons Villa were in the Championship, too. He was fouled a staggering 167 times during that 2019 – 2020 season; the second most fouled player in Premier League history was Jason Roberts in the 2002 - 2003 season. During the 2018 – 2019 season, he was also the most fouled player in any league – 149 times. Even in the 22 games during the 2020 – 2021 season he played in up to his injury in February 2021, he was fouled 99 times. The most surprising stat though was there were only around five bookings made for those 167 fouls. That's staggering! What does that suggest? The officials aren't protecting Jack, maybe? He must have been frustrated at that – he must have had bruises all over his shins and his side. Villa manager Dean Smith told the Telegraph, "There is nothing Jack can do other than wanting to keep getting on the ball and run at them in the final third. He loves playing the game and he loves Aston Villa, so he'll keep going."

The lack of 'proper' shinpads couldn't have helped; maybe that's why he's targeted by every other player in the league? "A few of the lads said that 'we've never seen anyone get kicked as much as you.

Getting kicked means, I'm doing something right most of the time," Jack said in a newspaper interview. It's a dangerous game, leaving your shins exposed to harsh tackles by opponents but according to Jack, he enjoys it. Luckily, Jack hasn't been deliberately injured in the shins yet.

Since making his debut for Villa at the end of the 2013 – 2014 Premier League season, Jack has had nine injuries which have resulted in him missing game time. Of those nine injuries, two have been shin related and two calf related. The injury that caused the most agony was the one he suffered before the busy Christmas period during the 2018 – 2019 Championship season. On that occasion he broke his shin and revealed the "horrific pain" he suffered after playing with it for two months until he broke down in the 87th minute at The Hawthorns on the 7th December 2018. Jack revealed to the Sun newspaper that he actually ignored the Villa doctor's advice, "I carried on playing — even though I wasn't really training throughout November and December. When we played West Brom at The Hawthorns, the pain in my shin was horrific. It turned out to be a fracture, which was sending pain into my ankle and the bottom of my left foot. Before the West Brom game I said, 'I don't think I'm going to be able to play'. The doc gave me an injection, it settled me down and I played until ten minutes from time. But that was the point when I thought, 'I can't carry on doing this', and went for a scan the next morning. I was on my way to London for our Christmas party when the doc rang — and he sounded low. He said, 'It's not good news. You've fractured your leg and you're not going to be able to play until March'. I said, 'Nah, I can play now but it's so painful — just give me a month and I'll be sorted'. But he said, 'You can't. If someone boots you, you've already fractured the bone. You could then have a major break to your leg and do some real damage to it'."

It was first thought that Jack would be back for the Sheffield United home game on the 8th February 2019, which seemed a bit premature, meaning he'd miss nine games; however, it wasn't to be, and he was out for another month.

Obviously, Jack did everything possible to get back fit as quick as he could but ultimately, it was rest that he needed, rest from getting his shins kicked in, week in, week out. He told the Express & Star newspaper that being out injured and spending most of your time doing rehab work in the gym can be a lonely process – no matter how much your team-mates try to keep you involved in all the camaraderie, "When you're injured, as much as everyone tries to make you feel part of it, you don't really (feel part of it) because you're not training or playing. I remember at the start the doctor was saying I could have days off over Christmas, but the manager wanted me to take part in team meetings about games. I've been taking part in most stuff, just not the training and the games."

By early March 2019, Jack returned after being out of action for three months, buoyed on by the fact Villa were still in with a (slim) chance of making the play-offs. He looked a whole lot stronger and even looked like he'd become a little leaner so he can carry the ball better. He had worked hard on the road to recovery once more and missing his football had just made him hungrier to succeed and get Villa to the play-offs. He knew deep down that everything was possible – this was the Championship, and anything goes.

Jack was given the added bonus of receiving the captain's armband and being considered the leader of his club, he must have been buoyed on even more by that. At last, Jack Grealish re-announced himself to the footballing world as one of the stand-out young English talents of his generation. How did he do that? Well, he only scored one of the goals of the season. After his time on the side-lines with a thunderous volley on the cusp of half-time against Derby County at Villa Park – and the rest is history.

****

Jack pulled out of training with a suspected shin injury and subsequently missed Villa's 2 – 1 home defeat to Leicester City on the 21st February 2021. It was initially thought he may be out for a maximum three weeks, but as the days and weeks passed, it became worrying, and Dean Smith continued to give little away. He was out for a period of three months.

On reflection, perhaps it's not the injuries that spur him on - maybe it's just that he misses playing football so much? One thing we as fans have learned about Jack Grealish since he appeared on the football scene is his ability to come back even better and stronger after receiving setbacks in his career - and even when there are no setbacks, he's consistently improving his game.

Let's face it, Jack Grealish has not had an easy career as a footballer to date; it's not been without controversy, injury, heartache and much more. However, each time he suffers a setback, he doesn't retreat into the depths of his own footballing ability, but he takes the setback for all it is worth, and it seems to fuel him and spur him on even more. Every footballer suffers injuries during their careers, some more than others, and some suffer horrific ones at that, and some never truly recover. This is one of the pitfalls of football.

The best quote from Jack to back this up was, "I worked so hard to come back because I missed football. I wanted to be the best I could be. I was in the gym every day." I think that sums up just what a driven person he is.

Chapter 10

JACK GREALISH - ANOTHER 'GAZZA'?

A lot of pundits have compared Jack Grealish to Paul Gascoigne, but is that a fair comparison?

No English player in recent times has excited football fans as much as Jack Grealish, and there has been comparisons with "Gazza", the maverick footballer that is Paul Gascoigne, which I find somewhat strange in a way. I say strange because "Gazza" was a very different player to Jack in many ways, and definitely a very different character.

We have seen a few false dawns when it comes to talented footballers arriving on the scene. We can think of someone like Jack Wilshere who easily springs to mind in recent times. At the age of 18 he was seemingly destined to become the 'next 'Gazza" after his excellent performances for Arsenal; we all thought he would kick on and be something very special. If it wasn't for his appalling injury record he may have done? Other players spring to mind, in the way of Joe Cole, David Bentley, Dele Alli and Ross Barkley, all very talented individuals who have since flattered to deceive.

Apparently, a few former managers and players have compared Jack with Paul Gascoigne, who also had to prove to his manager, Sir Bobby Robson that his unpredictable talent could be harnessed within a club side before going on to play for England. You had Glenn Hoddle, another ex-player of some repute, and an ex-England manager who could have gone onto great things saying, not only could Jack become the next 'Gazza', but also Phil Foden and James Maddison could too, "It comes back to that experience of playing. I think there are goals in Foden as well. Grealish has got good talent, Maddison has as well. Mason Mount, what he is doing ahead of say Grealish is playing Champions League football."

Bryan Robson was a great player and leader for Manchester United and England. However, his comments in the media about Jack went a bit over the top in my opinion, as he said, "No English player in recent years has excited me as much as Grealish does" while comparing him to Paul Gascoigne at some length. Without being unkind to Robson, let's not forget that this was the same person who compared Jack's Villa team-mate Ross Barkley in 2016 to 'Gazza', "Then we have Barkley who, like Wilshere, can provide something special. And I think a competition like this could just make him – he could become our new 'Gazza'."

If Robson got a bit carried away with comparing Barkley to 'Gazza', then he went the full hog when he spoke about Jack to Goal.com in November 2020, "Just like Gascoigne, he has got so much instinctive ability. He's got quick feet, can ghost past people and has good vision. Grealish is always on the front foot, always looking to create. It's what 'Gazza' loved doing, using his ability to go past defenders on both sides, scoring great goals, pleasing the crowd. And some of Grealish's goals have been outstanding. You can see that, just like 'Gazza', he loves what he's doing in being able to manipulate the ball. Grealish has got that natural ability the same as 'Gazza'. It's what sets them apart from the rest. 'Gazza's strength was to go past players on either side. He had this unbelievable knack of pushing you in the chest, then accelerating away from you — by actually fouling you first. Grealish does it differently but it's the same result and can be devastating. He's got massive leg muscles, calf muscles especially and that makes him very quick. That allows him to go either side and then like 'Gazza' did, he's away. It's the little things, the minor things if you like, that are really important to be a top player. They are minor but they are magic because other people can't do it. 'Gazza' had that special magic about him in the way he could get away from people. Grealish has that too."

Those comments made by 'Captain Marvel' himself, (Bryan Robson) got people talking and it also got a response from Jack, talking after he inspired England to a victory against Iceland in November 2020, he told the Telegraph about the comparisons, "Of course I know about 'Gazza'. I don't really see myself as him, but would love to be like him, the way that he played football. He played with such joy. I think everyone who watched him could see that. That is what I want to do. One of the biggest complements for people to say to is that you make them happy watching football. I would love to get compared to 'Gazza'. I think he is an absolute icon. Along with Wayne Rooney, he was probably one of the greatest England players over the last 30 years. There have been a load (of good players), but if they were the top two, 'Gazza' would be my first. I love 'Gazza', I've watched his documentary on Netflix a million times. I thrive off those kinds of comparisons. I love the way he played football with all the freedom and all the joy... I want to entertain people but I always want to be effective on the pitch like 'Gazza' was too. As you get older, you learn you are a hero to a lot of people and you are a role model. I've got to take it in my stride, and I'm just loving my life." Not getting too carried away, Jack then played down the comparisons, "Them comparisons are far away, I haven't played a tournament like he has. He thrived on the biggest stage and until I do that I can't be compared to him."

That response from Jack tells me he has the maturity and level-headedness not to let those comparisons go to his head, and he probably knows himself he's not Paul Gascoigne in disguise. Jack Grealish is, well Jack Grealish. That was backed up by Jack's Villa manager, Dean Smith who said Jack still has a long way to go before he can be compared to Gascoigne. Smith faced 'Gazza' in his playing days when 'Gazza' was at Everton. He could see why his Villa captain was being mentioned alongside 'Gazza' because of his unique playing style but warned everyone he is only at the start of his international career, "I played against Gascoigne; he was an unbelievable player. They are a long way off. Jack is five games into his England career. I see Jack as a unique player and because Paul was too I think that's why he is being compared."

I think one of the differences between the two includes the word 'unpredictable'? 'Gazza' was just that, unpredictable on the pitch and even more so off it; unpredictable in the sense you didn't know what he was going to do at any one time because he had the ability to outwit the opposition. Although you wouldn't call Jack Grealish 'predictable' in what he does on the pitch, he is more consistent with the way he plays, whereas with 'Gazza', the opposition couldn't handle him because of his unpredictability.

So, I've already suggested 'Gazza' was 'unpredictable' on and off the pitch, but he was also very much a 'maverick' footballer (and a 'maverick' person); some would call him a 'genius' of his day. Jack is a natural footballer, probably the best of his generation, and maybe he's a 'maverick' footballer, but I wouldn't call him a 'genius' in the mould of Paul Gascoigne, which isn't being disrespectful to Jack, but it's an observation from someone who watched 'Gazza' play for England, Tottenham and in Italy during the 1990s. Jack is a gifted footballer who trains hard, and puts in the extra miles and wants to improve, which tells you a lot about him as a person, but with 'Gazza' even if he didn't train for six weeks, he could go onto a football pitch and perform to a high standard, as if he had trained all week.

He certainly was a 'one-off'.

Is it fair to call 'Gazza' a football 'genius'? As the definition goes I guess there's an argument to be had; certainly, on his day he was. In football terms, there are 'good players' and 'very good players'. There are 'great players'. Then you have a handful of players who fall into another category, a special category that considers their charisma and the excitement they bring to a football match; their skills and innovation bring something fresh and unique that few players ever achieve. These players are called 'genius' players, and include George Best, Pele, Maradona, Messi and Ronaldo. Whether 'Gazza' falls into that category is up for debate, because he really was intermittent with his performances, unlike the other names I've mentioned, who were / are consistent week in, week out. Jack talks about Wayne Rooney, now there's a talent who could be classed as a 'great player' and was more consistent than 'Gazza' but he wasn't a 'genius' by any stretch of the imagination, which isn't being disrespectful to Wayne, because he was an outstanding talent. His England record speaks for itself. So, whether 'Gazza' was a 'genius' is for personal opinion, but comparing him to Best, Pele, and others maybe stretching it a bit.

So, comparing Jack to 'Gazza' even, when you look at the facts, is stretching the imagination way too far.

While I'm not sure I can see much of 'Gazza' in Jack Grealish, it could be said that there are some similarities between the two, but to compare them is unfair. Firstly, 'Gazza' was very pleasing on the eye, so is Jack; 'Gazza' always liked to get on the front foot, so does Jack, and 'Gazza' used to glide past defenders, and that is Jack's trademark. Where 'Gazza' had the natural ability to play in a multitude of positions in the England team of the 1990s, Jack also has that in his locker too, and that quality sets both of them apart from the rest.

However, the one thing that separates Jack apart from 'Gazza' is the ability to keep his head while on the pitch. Jack's temperament was put into question when he first arrived on the scene but he has learned and developed a superb level-headedness that, quite frankly, 'Gazza' probably never had. 'Gazza' would get himself into trouble and couldn't control his aggressive nature, whereas Jack seems to keep it all in, even though he gets kicked around the park every week. In other words, Jack is more mentally aware than 'Gazza' ever was – I don't think 'Gazza' was ever that intelligent anyway to be mentally aware, and even Sir Bobby Robson once described him as "Daft as a brush", but that's my own opinion.

Something that made Paul Gascoigne famous and loved by the adoring fans was his ability to 'play the fool' – he really wasn't the stereotypical footballer. He always had that childlike instincts to play tricks on his team-mates and generally not take life too seriously. Whereas Jack never looks to 'play the fool' and takes his role as captain of Villa seriously and takes gives every game the same respect that it deserves.

'Gazza' was the playmaker of that Bobby Robson team that almost went all the way to the World Cup Final in 1990, Jack can be the dazzling playmaker of Gareth Southgate's Euro 2021 team – given the chance.

For me, Paul Gascoigne was the best footballer I have ever seen wear an England shirt. He was an incredible player and he had everything in his locker. Unpredictability, entertainment value, personality, strength, scoring spectacular goals and the art of dribbling past players. In five or six-years' time, I'd love to say the same thing about Jack Grealish, and if he carries on in the rich vein of form he's been in for three or four seasons for Aston Villa, that will be a distinct possibility. Of course, we are talking about two players who played in different eras, but football is a simple game made complicated by tactics, and for me that's the difference between football of the 1990s and football of 2021 - but that's another debate.

For me, Jack has the talent to be a key cog for England for many years to come and although Gareth Southgate has hesitated to pick him until recently, I do think he will become important, when it comes to competitive games. He has shown the right mentality and maturity required since being made captain of Villa. That extra onus and responsibility has paid dividends to Jack and his performances have been consistent. It is unknown whether he can go up a level and perform on a major European stage, or even internationally in a tournament.

Even England manager, Gareth Southgate weighed into the argument, speaking at a pre-match press conference, when he said, "I am very conscious that I don't want to dampen the enthusiasm for Jack. I always answer honestly about people and when you talk about Gascoigne, there's not a player in English football history who was at that level in my opinion. I don't want that to be a criticism of Jack. I just think Gascoigne, who I played with, and I played with [Wayne] Rooney, [Steven] Gerrard, [Paul] Scholes, [David] Beckham and you could go on about phenomenal, amazing attacking players who won Champions Leagues, won 100 caps with England and who broke goalscoring records. In many ways, I feel Gascoigne was so unique, and such an incredible player that I feel like I am talking about Bobby Moore. I think with young players who come through you shouldn't burden or tag them by comparing them to someone else. Each one is unique with unique talents. Jack has a style that is different to all those players I have mentioned and all the players in our squad. He handled the question maturely and I understand the comparison but I think Gascoigne, as an individual is just on another level to anything I played with."

I think Gareth explained that very well indeed.

As I've said previously, we have seen many English players been hyped up to the hilt, then the embers extinguished before they had truly got off the ground. Although we don't know what the future holds for Jack I truly think he will buck the trend and become even better than he is at 26 years old. As for comparisons with 'Gazza' or anyone else, he must now concentrate and establish himself and carve out his own niche as a performer in his own right. Of course, the bigger the stage, the more attention he will receive and it will be up to him how he handles it, but judging from the start he made for England, I don't think that will be a problem, because he has said himself, he can handle the pressure, attention and the fame that comes with being a professional footballer.

Wouldn't it have been great if 'Gazza' was playing today, so we could compare the two, like-for-like? That's another reason why I said it's not fair to compare the two players, because they played in different eras.

However, if there was anyone Jack reminds me of, it isn't "Gazza", but maybe Andrés Iniesta in his prime. the movement of his shoulders, his pace and the ability to skip past players is reminiscent of the former Barcelona midfield legend. I'm not saying Jack is at that level yet, but in the way he plays it could be compared to the great Spanish superstar.

Jack Grealish definitely has the qualities required to survive and become his own man and his destiny is entirely in his own hands (and feet), and he has the talent to be as good as Paul Gascoigne, even if he's not 'the new 'Gazza''.

Chapter 11

THE INSPIRATIONS AND INFLUENCES THAT DRIVE JACK

What inspires Jack to be the player he has become and what makes him tick?

The drive that inspires Jack Grealish is more than just to play in the Champions League, World Cups and Euros, although those are the ultimate draw for him in terms of the level he wants to play at.

Many kids dream of becoming a footballer, let alone a famous one, following in the footsteps of their heroes. For Jack Grealish, he was once that kid watching on the touchlines at Villa Park, dreaming he'd be the 'next Juan Pablo Angel' or the 'next Paul Merson', and dreaming of the day he'd be playing for Villa. Now, over 20 years later, it's role reversal for Jack, who now looks at the kids looking at him from the side-lines, and them dreaming about being the 'next Jack Grealish'. Jack describes it as a "dream come true", and he said, "It makes me happy when I'm warming up, seeing the kids there."

However, how many of them have a story that lies underneath their motivation to be get to the top? There are some fantastic stories behind the world's best footballers, no greater than Lionel Messi, for instance, who suffered from severe growth hormone deficiency when he was young and can you believe that it affected his ability to score goals? His family couldn't afford to pay for treatment, so when Barcelona discovered him, his father told the club that his son would only sign for them if they paid for his treatment. Guess what? Barcelona duly obliged and Messi arguably became 'the world's best footballer' of his generation and mentioned in the same conversations as Maradona and Pele.

Neymar is another interesting story, as he faced sheer poverty and an unprivileged upbringing; his family had no electricity in their house and his father had to have three jobs to make ends meet. Now, he's one of the most famous footballers on the planet.

Luka Modric grew up in a dingy hotel amid a war zone back in his homeland of Croatia. He has now overcome the adversities and his lack of confidence to become one of the best midfielders in the world.

The list goes on, and the stories are plentiful.

So, just what is the inspirational story behind Jack Grealish and what motivates him to become as good as his is?

Aston Villa were in the semi-final of the FA Cup and were playing Bolton Wanderers at Wembley on Sunday 2nd April 2000, 90 minutes that wouldn't live in the memories of Villa fans for as long as the game itself was forgetful, although they progressed to the final after beating the Lancashire team on penalties. However, for the Grealish family, it wouldn't be a day that they would remember for the football, but for a family tragedy that would rock their world.

Jack was a 4-year-old boy on that day, a day that would change his life forever; however, unbeknown to him back then, it would be the day he would look back on and think about every day of his life.

Jack's father, Kevin had been in London to watch the cup tie but received news that his baby son, Keelan had tragically died due to cot death, so missed the game and rushed back to Solihull to be with his family. He told the Birmingham Mail, "I remember being told what had happened to Keelan when I was down there for the match and I rushed back. He was only nine months old; he was a little angel, and I was devastated. We all were."

No one can ever understand how a parent feels when they lose a child; people can sympathise and give their love, but the parent's own feelings are very personal. It is something the Grealish family will never get over; however, according to Kevin, they are grateful and blessed that they have two more sons and two daughters who will always think of Keelan.

It is sometimes said that 'out of every tragedy there comes new strength' and following the sadness of losing Keelan, the Grealish family set a task to raise money for a cot death charity through a sponsored abseil and a raffle – they raised an amazing £6,500 for that charity. Aston Villa FC donated one of the playing shirts from the game and Kevin paid £260 for it in an auction. He had "KEELAN" and the number "1" printed on the back of it.

The legacy of Keelan's death lives on to this day. Kevin revealed to the Birmingham Mail how one of the first trophies Jack ever won as a young player was donated to his school in Keelan's honour. The cup was given to Jack's primary school, Our Lady of Compassion Roman Catholic School in Solihull for use in their house competitions, and would you believe, Jack even won the cup that took his brother's name, "He won a cup with one of the boys teams he used to play for when he was seven or eight," recalled Kevin, "You should have seen the size of it - it was like the European Cup! The team manager asked if anybody wanted to keep it and because Jack had done well in the tournament, he let us have it. We decided to give it to Jack's school for them to give out on sports days and things like that. They called it the 'Keelan Daniel Grealish Memorial Cup' which was a nice touch and as far as I know they still have it."

Although Jack was only four years old himself when he lost his brother, he still remembers him and thinks about him with everything he does. Kevin told the Birmingham Mail, "I said to Jack when I remember the last FA Cup semi-final against Bolton and the news we got that day, and then I think about what he achieved and the way he played against Liverpool, he made us so proud and brought us so much happiness."

To this day, every ball that Jack kicks he is motivated by the death of his brother and he is driven by the desire to honour his memory for his parents. All through his career to date, Jack has paid his respects to Keelan, and in fact, dedicated his first senior goal he scored for Notts County in the 2013 – 2014 season against Gillingham to his baby brother, "I like to dedicate my special stuff to him," he told the Birmingham Mail, "When I scored in the NextGen I dedicated my goals to him so hopefully I can do that again in the first team and make him proud. I was only young when he died, and it was so sad. It taught me to enjoy my life, that's what you have got to do. It was a horrible time for my parents, but this is where we are now, and my aim is just to make them all proud."

The last time Aston Villa played their local rivals, Birmingham City in the 'Second City derby' was on Sunday 10th March 2019. That day was marred by the disgraceful thug who ran on the pitch and blatantly attacked Jack. Then in the 67th minute, Jack scored the winner to send the visiting fans home in ecstasy. However, what those fans probably didn't realise at the time was that Jack dedicated that goal to his baby brother and was reduced to tears amid those passionate celebrations, "I had tears in my eyes. I was crying because all my family were there and it's a moment I dreamed of as a fan. I got emotional after scoring because of my little brother who passed away. I dedicated the goal to him. Ever since I was a little kid at school, these were the games I dreamed of playing in, but to score brings it to another level and it is probably the favourite moment of my career so far."

For me, that story is every bit as emotional and inspiring as Messi's, Neymar's or Modric's stories. I think you can now see what makes some of the best footballers tick and try and improve every day. That drive and motivation is both inspiring and commendable.

With Villa having their best Premier League season for over a decade and Jack's outstanding performances during the 2020 – 2021 season, especially at the start of the season, Paul Merson, a former Villa player who was an early inspiration for Jack, described his performances as being "on another planet", which was praise indeed coming from Merse. Even though Jack must take pleasure in all the plaudits heaped on him, he apparently remained down to earth and never let it all become a distraction. He spoke to Matt Maher at the Express & Star newspaper, "I still think there is so much more to come from me and that is not being big-headed either.

It is just having confidence in my own ability. I think everyone I have worked with will say how confident I am as a person and as a player in my own ability. I truly believe in myself and think I have so much more to give. I have big aims for this season (2020 – 2021). Of course, it is nice to hear those things, particularly from people like Paul Merson and Gary Lineker. But you never want to listen to it too much, to the point it starts to affect you. You just have to take it, move on and then try to do more to earn even more praise. That is what I try to do. I know what I can give. I know what I can do as a player."

In the modern game, footballers increasingly use stats as a motivational tool, and Jack Grealish is no different. I have previously highlighted the outstanding stats for the 2020 – 2021 season up to the time he got injured, which included being involved in scoring or assisting 15 goals in the first 19 Premier League games, a statistic Jack placed particular focus on, improving his final ball. As Jack has progressed as a footballer, he has turned to other inspirations, other players to watch and one of them Jack revealed was Manchester City midfielder, Kevin De Bruyne. He told the 2020 League Cup Final matchday programme, "Kevin De Bruyne is my favourite player in the Premier League at the moment. I try to base my game on his."

In the age of television and tools like YouTube, it's easy for people to watch almost anything and anyone, even on their phone. Jack spoke to Sky News after his impressive performances at the beginning of his England international career by saying, "For the past 24 hours, I've been watching little clips of my favourite players like I do before every game. I watch loads of clips. I watch clips of De Bruyne, I watch clips of Coutinho, just players that are in my position, really. That's what I've done since I was a little kid and I still do it to this day – I have no shame in saying that and that's what gets me going for football matches." It has certainly worked wonders. Jack explained to Matt Maher, "Half of it is watching. You watch players like Kevin De Bruyne and when he gets into the final third, what he does. You need to mix it up, sometimes dink to the back stick, sometimes go underneath the defence. You need to mix it up as much as possible. That is what I have been doing in training and it has paid off in the matches."

Inspiration and motivation comes in various forms for different people. Everyone knows that Jack has been the most fouled and most targeted player in both the Championship and the Premier League for several seasons, and he revealed to the Express & Star that he loves it when people target him, both on and off the pitch. So where does he get that from, being able to cut out the verbal abuse from opposing fans and the physical torment he receives on the pitch? "I love all that," Grealish said. "I love when people are on my back and targeting me." Jack suggested he was inspired and influenced by watching Cristiano Ronaldo, "I always remember when I was a kid — and I am not saying I am anywhere near his level — but Cristiano Ronaldo (when he played for Manchester United) used to come to Villa and the fans used to absolutely cane him. He used to thrive off it and that is what I try to do. I try to thrive off the hatred from the fans."

In an interview with **www.talentaintenough.co.uk,** Jack said that Ronaldo has been his biggest influence on his career to date, "I used to watch him when I was young, he was quite skinny at the time (at Manchester United), completely different to the way he is now, and over the years, just watching him develop and watching him change, he's obviously been a standout for anyone to watch. Everyone's seen what he's gone on to do in his career and for me, that's what I look to and aspire to because that's the way I see myself, when I was younger that's what I needed to do; do stuff in the gym, do stuff off the pitch and I feel like it's helped me, just like it's helped him."

I've already mentioned the influence of his father on Jack, and in the same interview, he revealed that his father used to tell him to always enjoy himself and play with a smile on his face and you can see that in his game – nothing seems to faze Jack, and he's always smiling, which is good to see.

Those two interviews gave a real insight into the mind of Jack Grealish and what motivates and inspires him to improve in each game. It appears he really is a 'football nut' and wants to be the best. He's also not afraid of anything or anyone, which is a sign he has an abundance of self-confidence required to be a top footballer in the modern era.

What makes Jack the player he has become? Well, you only need to look at Jack's physique, which is unusual, one would have to say (in a good way). You can see how much he has worked on his body in recent years - his upper body strength and his legs, especially. Take his legs for instance. They are bulging with muscle, and he now has a reputation of having enormous calves, as I've previously stated, that are a source of public debate; they are also the root of his footballing strength. The strength of his legs gives him an edge over other players, a physical edge over even most of the finely tuned Premier League athletes of 2021.

The calf muscle is crucial for Jack's game, to control acceleration and also to decelerate, which is all part of the way he plays. They are frequently referenced in television commentary, too, as a light-hearted distraction from the seriousness of the game. On a light-hearted note, Dean Smith quipped at the end of the 2019 – 2020 season that there must be "a lot of girls out there who are admiring Jack's calves," but those muscles are not just for show — they are fundamental to his movement as an athlete, and to his success on the pitch. His game is about slowing down his opponents, then exploding instantaneously; his game isn't about taking off with the ball, like wingers for instance, it's more about hesitating, slowing the game down, then taking advantage of his pace. His huge calves help him control that instant change in pace and direction.

You can see Jack's body is built for brilliance. His stomach, the core strength makes him more solid and powerful and helps him maintain balance when he changes direction. His thigh muscles make him more resilient and capable of coping with repeated fouling, one thing that he has had to get used to for four or five seasons. The strength of his legs helps him manage the weight of his upper body. I've mentioned a lot about his calves, but with the power of them he can be on his toes as he plays, which allows him to be light on his feet and help his instant reactions.

According to Jack, he told *talentaintenough.co.uk* that the effort he puts in now at the gym has helped him develop his game, "When I was young, I was getting knocked off the ball, getting kicked, still do, but now I don't really mind it. At 16 or 17 I thought that my talent could do all the talking and there came a point when I went to the

Championship and it was tough there, a lot of stronger, quicker players than myself, and when I got injured when I was 21 or 22, that was a real turning point for me. I needed to do stuff in the gym, doing more strength programmes, upper body stuff; that was when I was getting knocked off the ball a fair bit, and everything changed then. Since then, I've been doing gym work twice a week and it helps me. Obviously in the Premier League you've got to be fit, you've got to be strong to compete against the best players in the world. I'm certainly doing that now and I'm getting the rewards for it. When I'm carrying the ball, that's when I need my strength and pace, my stamina and everything I do off the pitch, gym wise all helps and all relates to it."

People talk a lot about a footballer's inspiration, hunger and desire; some people can question a few players that they don't have any, but nobody can ever question Jack Grealish as he has all three characteristics in abundance. Jack told Matt Maher, "I don't think I will ever lose this hunger. There is nothing I love doing more than entertaining people."

Dean Smith gave an insight how Jack has turned into an effective and responsible leader of his team since he was given the captain's armband, when he said, "He's pushing the other players now, that's the pleasing thing." Part of the credit can go to John Terry (JT), who has been Dean Smith's assistant for three years and himself, an inspirational captain of Chelsea and England. JT has apparently been a key source of inspiration and advice to Jack when developing his leadership skills, "You've got to (push people) as captain, especially at a club as big as Villa. We demand a lot from each other, as players. We are a young team and that is what I have tried to build on over the past year, the way I am off the pitch, being that leadership figure."

Being made captain of Aston Villa in March 2019 was obviously a great bonus for Jack and he says himself, that he can handle the added pressure, "I love being captain of this club, I just thrive off it. I've never really been one that when I have pressure on me I always think I play better. I've played in games for England; in big games for Villa against local rivals, I've always performed well. I think it's something to thrive off. A coach at Villa used to say, 'pressure is a privilege' and I've always remembered that. If anything, I love the pressure." I'm not sure if Jack ever wanted to become captain of Aston Villa, or even thought about it, but it was an inspiring choice that Dean Smith made and it has certainly inspired Jack to step his game up a notch or two, because he's the 'main man' now for his boyhood club, and that in itself can only inspire him even more to improve himself and his game.

According to Jack, it's been different being captain of a Championship club than one in the Premier League. He spoke to *Soccerbible* about the transition, "Obviously it's a big difference between the Championship where you're winning most games to then being in the Premier League, battling and not winning as many. I do now see myself as a leader in the dressing room. I'm still young but I class myself as one of the more experienced players and I think the whole team would too. As a leader, I wouldn't say I'm one of these captains that goes around screaming and shouting all the time. I'm not really like that. There's others on our team that do that. I like to lead by the way I play football. I think that's one of the reasons why the manager did make me captain."

Has it affected him being made captain? In an interview with the Express & Star, Jack suggested he's still fairly laid back, but he seems a whole lot more mature, especially when being interviewed, which he's done a lot of since he took the captain's armband, "The captaincy has changed my approach a little bit. Through my whole life I have always been laid back. It's little stuff, like when we were going to do warm-ups I would always be the one at the end, just jogging over last. Now because I'm captain I am the one at the front leading it, trying to get everyone motivated. That is probably the only way it has changed me. It is off the pitch more than anything else. I try to be more of a leader."

It seems Jacks is always challenging himself to do better, and he relishes being the 'main man' at Villa Park, "Sometimes I think the team look to me, not rely on me as such, but they do look to me if they need a goal and I love that. It is not a burden, not one bit. No matter how good or bad I am playing, I will always want the ball, in whatever situation. I thrive off that and fortunately I have been doing that recently."

Indeed, not many people know his true character away from the public image, but it can typically be seen a couple of hours after every home match by the gates of the players' car park, he's there meeting the fans and is generous with his time (in 'normal' times of course), "I'll go up into the box after the game and my dad will be there with about 50 programmes to sign for the kids outside. That is just the way my family are. They are nice and generous people. Being a local lad coming up through the ranks I have been the one on the other side of the gate, waiting for the players. I've been there and I know how much it means. It is important that we as players are role models and it is important we give the fans our time. A lot of the lads do it anyway, but the manager tells us as well. He is a Villa fan himself and has been in the same situation I have. We were both young and we adored Villa players. He tells us to make sure we speak to the fans because it is important. The club wouldn't be much without fans."

When you talk about what influences or inspires someone, a footballer for example, you normally talk about past or present players, but for Jack, a massive influence has been his manager, Dean Smith. Jack explained his managers' influence on the Peter Crouch Podcast, "I can't really give him enough praise. He gave me the armband and ever since then both of us haven't looked back. He's been excellent for me. Everyone reacts differently to types of managers; some people need an arm round their shoulder, some people need a kick up the backside. I can speak to him about anything. If I've got problems on or off the field, I can always speak to him. He likes to put his arm around my shoulder and help me and that's why I want to repay him." To have a manager like that and to have such a great rapport with him must be great for Jack and it must inspire him to do the very best he can for Dean Smith, which for any Villa fan, is all you want to hear.

Jack Grealish is a very interesting character indeed, one who has lots of inspirations, motivations and reasons for improving himself as a person and as a professional footballer. All of the above are a credit to him; his story is interesting and the reasons for wanting to be the very best are commendable. This will ultimately inspire younger people to be like him, to follow in his footsteps, just like he has followed in the footsteps of his footballing heroes.

Chapter 12

JACK'S HELPING HANDS

Little is known about Jack's charity work, but the Villa midfielder is more than just a brilliant footballer, he's a role model to thousands of fans, including those in need.

Everyone now knows the enormous class and talent Jack Grealish shows on the pitch, but little is known about what he does off the pitch.

While Aston Villa Football Club do much for charity via the Foundation, not many people know that Jack himself has shown his class off the pitch as well and helped out many people during his short football career and has done much to raise money for charity or more recently, the NHS.

For an outsider, it's quite amazing why famous footballers or other celebrities don't publicise their charity or fundraising work a lot more than they do (or don't); all that good work seems to go un-noticed and unreported in the mainstream media, or even social media, and that is a great shame.

Firstly, not many people know that Jack is one of a host of famous footballers who campaign for a charity called **Saving Lives**, who educate people about the importance of testing for HIV, Hepatitis B and C and other sexually transmitted infections. Jack is one of 24 Ambassadors from the world of football.

In this section, I have documented a timeline of some of the events

Jack has contributed to that have gone largely under the radar.

August 2016

Young Villa fan, Carter Carrington was born with Fibular Hemimelia and had his leg amputated at 11 months old and was eventually fitted with a prosthetic leg. He was only four years old when his father, Marlon, showed pictures on Twitter of his son's new prosthetic leg which had a Villa crest on his shin. That message was shown over 300 times before it was spotted by 19-year-old Jack. Moved by the pictures, Jack responded to the Tweet and promised to welcome Carter to Villa Park as a mascot and asked Carter to choose a game during that 2016 – 2017 Championship season.

Unbeknown to Jack, Carter's favourite player just happened to be...... well Jack, of course.

The game Carter chose was the Villa home fixture with Midlands rivals Nottingham Forest. Carter and his father travelled from their home in Bognor Regis to watch the game and Carter's dreams came true when he walked out onto the Villa Park pitch with his hero, Jack for the game on 11th September 2016. Carter's father told the Bognor Regis Observer, "He had an amazing day and weekend and loved spending time with Jack. I felt so proud watching him walking onto the pitch at Villa Park with 30,000 plus people cheering, although he was more interested in Bella the mascot at the time!"

November 2016

Ajay Moran-Nabi was missing his right hand above the wrist and mum Amanda approached 'Team UnLimbited', an organisation which designs, builds, fits and delivers 3D printed hands and arms to children in the UK completely free. Jack and his then Villa team-mate Jonathan Kodjia helped make a young fan's day during a special visit to the Bodymoor Heath training ground. Ajay, a 10-year-old Villa fan, was treated to a behind-the-scenes tour of the complex and afterwards was presented with his new claret and blue 3D prosthetic arm by Jack.

March 2017

Brave two-year toddler, Charlie Round touched many hearts during his short life, none more so than Jack Grealish. The inspirational lad sadly lost his fight against a rare cancer called Neuroblastoma in March 2017.

However, while young Charlie was fighting the disease, Jack kindly donated £515 towards his treatment and a tee-shirt he had worn during the warm-up ahead of the Norwich City game in February 2016.

April 2017

The Aston Villa Foundation is the official charity of the club and all the senior players have commitments to it. At the end of the 2016 – 2017 season, Jack was awarded the Aston Villa Community Champion by the Foundation.

When Jack received the award, he told the Aston Villa website, "I was absolutely delighted to be named the club's community Player of the Year. I'm extremely appreciative of my position as a footballer and the fact I'm able to get involved in good causes. Nothing compares to the look on a young supporter's face when they've received a surprise visit from a footballer." The head of the Foundation, Guy Rippon, was delighted that Jack won the award, "Jack received this award as he has repeatedly shown how he is happy to go above and beyond in terms of community and supporter engagement. He has demonstrated on several occasions this season how he brings a really personal touch to our community engagement. That's not just attending large events such as the JV-Life Christmas Party, but also taking time out to allow young supporters facing significant personal challenges to meet their hero individually and make them feel very special."

February 2018

Teenage Aston Villa 'superfan', Moin Younis, who suffers from a painful disease called Epidermolysis Bullosis, was made famous when he was pictured 'chilling out' with no other than David Beckham at the Pride of Britain Awards. Young Moin and his family were trying to raise £250,000 to fund costs towards his care and treatment. The BBC filmed a documentary about him and made a big impact. That's where Jack got involved. He and Gabby Agbonlahor galvanised the playing squad to help Moin and managed to raise £20,000 – and that was on top of what Jack had donated himself.

March 2019

14-year-old Leukaemia patient, Harrison Price received a boost when Jack was pictured presenting him with a number '40 Grealish' Villa shirt at his home in Solihull, West Midlands. Jack was a regular visitor to Harrison, and was welcomed into the house on many occasions, sometimes to play the video game, FIFA.

Some of Harrison's family and family friends had planned some events to support Cure Leukaemia, including a cycle ride at the Velodrome in Birmingham and a five-a-side football tournament. Harrison's mother told the Solihull Observer newspaper, "Jack has been really good for Harry because he does miss out on a lot of things that normal teenagers enjoy, but the friendship does make him very popular when he gets into school."

August 2019

'Super Jack' and the generosity of some Villa fans rallied round to support disabled Villa supporter, Ryan Epps to buy a special power wheelchair costing around £8,500. The chair helped make Ryan's life a bit easier as he was able to get around and give him more independence. Head of the Villa Foundation, Guy Rippon, told the Birmingham Mail, "As Villa fans always do they pick up the story, they crowd fund and raised £8,500 to buy the chair and Jack Grealish also contributed."

The club then invited Ryan to enjoy a behind-the-scenes tour around Villa Park in his new chair prior to the home game against Bournemouth on 17th August 2019 and he got to thank Jack for his help and generous donation of £1,500 towards the chair.

March 2020

With the national lockdown only days old, Jack was allegedly involved in a car crash after breaking the UK Government's 'Stay at Home' lockdown rules, "I knew straight away that I had to come out and apologise myself," the Times quoted Jack as saying, "I didn't want to hide behind a club statement. I'm old enough now and mature enough to know I'd done wrong. Since then, I've tried to keep my head down, work hard and do as much charitable work as possible."

With that in mind, Jack was apparently fined by the club and the estimated £150,000 proceeds were donated to The University Hospital's Charity in Birmingham.

April 2020

While the UK was in the grip of the Coronavirus pandemic and in full lockdown, Jack tried to do his bit and help the NHS in the battle against the virus that gripped the whole world. He decided to hold a raffle for the Villa shirt that he wore during the iconic 1 – 0 victory against Birmingham City at St Andrew's on Sunday 10th March 2019, the same game in which he was attacked on the pitch and later scored the winner.

Jack posted on his Instagram feed, *"To show my support to the NHS I'm holding a raffle for one of my favourite match day shirts, with the money raised going to the NHS Charities Together fund. Everyone knows how important that match was to me! This was a big win against our rivals and continued our march towards promotion."*

The charity raffle followed a similar thing organised by former Villa striker, Gabby Agbonlahor, *"A big shout out to my bro Gabby Agbonlahor who raised £17K. Gabby and I discussed this a couple of weeks back and we're really happy to be able to help."* He suggested on his JustGiving page that the raffle for shirt raised over £55,000 for the NHS Charities Together, with over 3,600 people donating to the cause. Jack was quoted as saying, "I know I'm a footballer but I'm still human and we all make mistakes. I'm also a role model as well to a lot of people out there, especially young children who might look up to me. I try to act in a respectable manner."

May 2020

After an Aston Villa fan revealed on Twitter that he was raising money for a mental health charity following news that his best friend had committed suicide in May 2020, after a long battle with mental health issues, Jack stepped in and offered to donate a signed Villa shirt from the 2018 – 2019 promotion season to raise money for the charity. *"Terrible news,"* wrote Jack on his Twitter feed, *"I will donate one of my shirts from last season which is also signed by the promotion winning team from last season."* The proceeds went to the NHS Charities Together.

September 2020

"I literally just put the page up and then my mum was on the family group saying, 'Have you seen what he's donated?' I was, like, 'Who?' She said, 'Jack.' Obviously, I went on the page and saw how much he had donated. I think it's absolutely incredible." Jack's former Villa team-mate, Lewis Kinsella told Sky Sports after he launched a fundraising page to help his club, Aldershot cover the costs of a knee operation.

As soon as Jack saw the appeal, he donated £2,000 to support his mate, "I never expected him to donate as much as he did. Me and Jack obviously go back a long time and have stayed in touch ever since I left. We always speak. I went to watch him at Wembley. We are good friends, but I did not ask him, I did not pre-warn him or anything."

September 2020

David Quainton, a 73-year-old Villa fan from Oxfordshire, was sent a signed Villa away shirt by Jack through his son, Mark, who reached out to the Villa captain in an attempt to lift his father's spirits. David had been battling cancer since 2013 so Mark wrote to Jack on Twitter and to his amazement, received a Direct Message back from a cousin of Jack's, asking for Mark's number, "Half an hour later, Jack's dad called, and we've been staying in regular contact, he asks how dad is and how he's getting on." Mark told the Oxford Mail, "Dad's really happy with the shirt, as obviously Jack gets a lot of messages and requests. Things like this give him a boost and put a smile on his face. There is a possibility Jack might visit or he'll give us a call at some point, once we get through the beginning of the new football season and depending on what lockdown restrictions there are."

November 2020

With COVID19 affecting the distribution of the new PlayStation 5 games console during its launch in November 2020, Jack decided to help a young Villa fan and Pride of Britain winner, Moin Younis, who suffers from a rare genetic skin disorder by gifting him a signed console. Young Moin, who I've mentioned previously, took to Twitter and asked if anyone had took delivery of the console on launch day. Jack, who had been in contact with Moin for a few years, let the 20-year Mo's plea go unnoticed and sent him a signed console with a personal message written on the box. It read: *"To my brother Moin, a little early Christmas present for ya!! Enjoy bro. Love ya mate, from Jacky 10."* Moin captioned the image with the reply, *"Just had this delivered and a little message from Villa captain @ jackgrealish. Can't believe life right now. Thank you soooo much bro I can't even tell you on post how much I appreciate this."*

The two first met back in 2017 and he donated £1,500 alongside other players to aid his battle against Epidermolysis Bullosa. Jack told AVTV in late November 2020, "I speak to Mo a lot, I've got a sister who's disabled, so I can relate when I go to the Children's Hospital. I'm not saying you have to have someone disabled to be able to relate, but me more than anyone knows what it's like. My sister has so many idols, she just loves Kirk from Coronation Street and I've got Kirk's number and I FaceTime him now and again with my little sister and it makes her day. When I have the chance to be able to do this for certain people I do try and Mo was obviously asking me for a while, saying 'Is there anyone who can get me a PlayStation for me?', he obviously wasn't asking for it for free, he just couldn't get one because they were sold out everywhere. I managed to buy one for him, and I didn't even tell him, I actually messaged Gabby Agbonlahor and asked him 'can you get me Mo's address because I want to drop this to his house'. I was just in training and the PlayStation come and I was buzzing because I thought I'd go and pop to his after training. I got outside and rang his doorbell (I didn't go inside obviously) and left the PlayStation there for him. I waited in my car and he was absolutely over the moon. When you can help people, especially people like Mo who suffer day-to-day, it just means the world to me to be able to be put in a position where I can help them. I think us as footballers can do it so much more."

December 2020

Aston Villa FC arranged a series of virtual meet-ups over the festive period of 2020, and one of them involved Jack making surprise calls to give a boost to families who have been going through challenging times. One of those who received a call from the Villa captain was eight-year-old Bowie Rix, who has a rare genetic condition called Bohring-Opitz syndrome. The condition means Bowie has developmental delay, communication problems, severely limited mobility as well as other issues. Jack delighted Bowie's Villa-supporting family by calling up for a chat, taking questions from the family and talking about his own experiences of having a sister who has cerebral palsy. After the call, Jack promised to meet up with Bowie and his family at Villa Park once supporters were allowed back at the ground.

February 2021

Mia Craen from Horsham, Sussex was an avid Aston Villa fan and a massive sports fan and competitor. Sadly, the 18-year-old lost her life when she drove home one day in early February 2021 and her car collided into a tree. Mia's favourite player was of course, Jack and that inspired her friend, Rosie Fletcher to write on his Instagram page, **"Given that she was a huge @avfcofficial and @jackgrealish fan, we would like to get recognition for Mia and the amazing person she was."** Friends were encouraged to tag Jack's Instagram account and followers were asked to make donations. Jack duly obliged by donating no less than £2,000 to Mia's funeral costs, while he also sent a personal message of condolences to her brother, Finlay Craen.

Finlay's GoFundMe page raised nearly £20,000 for Mia's funeral.

****

Due to the COVID-19 restrictions in the UK over the Christmas period in 2020, footballers, including Villa players, weren't allowed do their usual visits to hospitals and hospices to see kids like Mo. Jack told AVTV, "The lads will tell you, if you speak to any of them, how much we just love doing it and we go there and it's so nice to be able to put a smile on all the kids' faces and see how much it means to them, us going in there and dropping them presents and signing stuff for them. It's going to be hard this year (Christmas 2020) not being able to do that but fingers crossed we can sort something out and make a few children happy this Christmas."

Chapter 13

ENGLAND: THE DREAM COMES TRUE

"A dream come true to receive my first senior call up for @England"

England head coach, Gareth Southgate has had a history of promoting youngsters into his England set-up, but he took some convincing to call up Jack Grealish into the fold.

After several years of speculation, Jack finally made his decision to dedicate his international football career to the country of his birth in September 2015. However, Jack had to wait almost another FIVE years before he finally got his call-up to the England squad by the now manager, Gareth Southgate. During those five years, the biggest question surrounding Jack Grealish and England has always been, is he ready?

On 31st August 2020, that question was finally answered.

Ironically, Jack had hoped Gareth Southgate's promotion from Under-21 manager to senior manager in 2016 would have helped his cause, given Jack played under him for the Under-21s. He talked about his time with Gareth Southgate and the Under-21s in 2016, "Our team was so together, and that's partly because of Gareth. He gives all the boys confidence. You can see the England first-team doing well under him. I'm trying to keep my place with the 21s, hopefully go to the European Championships next summer (Euro 2016) and then try and get into the first team. I feel in the future I can go and play for England. That's definitely my target. That's my dream."

It wasn't until the squad was announced by Southgate for a double-header Nations League games against Iceland and Denmark on 31st August 2020 that the growing number of followers clamouring for Jack's long-awaited inclusion were silenced. Even Prince William, The Duke of Cambridge himself, got in on the act, joking to The Peter Crouch Podcast after Southgate's previous squad announcement in July 2020 omitted the Villa star again, "Gareth (Southgate) is a legend, I really like Gareth and I think he's doing a great job with the England team, that's not to say that conversations haven't been had where I give him a little nudge and say: 'Why isn't (Jack) Grealish in the England squad?'"

Villa fans had been waging almost a war-footing against the England manager ever since Jack made his long-awaited announcement in September 2015. The ever-critical media had been questioning the England manager's decisions ever since. Even though Villa had been struggling in the Premier League and were finally relegated in the following season (2015 – 2016). Jack then played three seasons in the Championship. Becoming a star in his own right. Even when Villa made it back to the Premier League, it wasn't a foregone conclusion that he would get the nod from the former Villa skipper Southgate. However, Villa's faithful fans were eagerly waiting with baited-breath news of his promotion to the national side, but that wait was longer than anyone expected.

I don't think anyone doubted Jack's talent, none more so than former England manager, Roy Hodgson, who said he never doubted the star quality of Jack Grealish, and even helped persuade him to pledge his international allegiance to England, "I always believed in him. It's very different going back five years to a very much younger Jack Grealish and someone just starting his rise to the top," Hodgson told Four-Four-Two magazine in late 2020, "I have been impressed by the constant improvement over the years and in particular, the last two seasons. I thought last season (2019 – 2020) he was very good and showed a different maturity and level to his game. If anything, he has kicked on even further this year. Now he's the first name on everyone's lips when you are preparing for a match against Aston Villa, he's somebody you know you are going to have to try and stop - or at least limit, the creative passes he's going to inflict during the game."

Whether or not Gareth Southgate thought Jack was ready for that step up was pure guesswork, but the Villa fans and a growing list of football 'pundits' were left perplexed after every England squad was announced, minus Jack Grealish's name. It wasn't only Gareth Southgate though who failed to pick Jack, but Roy Hodgson and Sam Allardyce before him decided not to take a chance on him. However, it seemed Southgate got the brunt of the criticism because he had been England manager for much longer. It left the fans wondering what he had to do to get picked. Back when Villa were in the Championship, the England manager challenged Jack that he needed to be playing in the Premier League if he wanted to make his senior debut, which I found a bit unfair. He was playing in a very physical league and was out-performing anyone else. Younger players like Declan Rice, Callum Hudson-Odoi, Jadon Sancho and Phil Foden seemed to overtake Jack in the pecking order as they had been playing for their clubs in the top league on a regular basis. No one can doubt that Gareth Southgate has given youth a chance since he became the England national manager, with two 18-year-olds in Rice and Hudson-Odoi both featuring in one England team in recent times, the first time in 138 years that has ever happened.

Southgate is obviously an admirer of Jack and was quoted in the Telegraph as saying, "Jack worked with us in the Under-21s briefly. The difficulty is always, although we can see the quality, when the evidence of the opponent is a different level, that's where it's hard to directly correlate what that is going to look like at a level above. With Callum Hudson-Odoi, he's playing Europa League, he's playing Premier League, that does make a difference." For Villa fans, those words only fuelled the fire because they knew that their man was good enough to put on that white shirt of England.

Southgate then went on to justify his stance, then contradicted what he'd previously said, "I'm not going to say we won't pick a player from the Championship because that could happen but it's far more difficult to assess his level. You see certain parts of the game but not others. Not the physicality at times, nor the tactical discipline. That's another level in the Premier League: the speed, the pace. So, he's (Jack) a player we know all about, he's a player we track. But that last bit of evidence that could give you confidence to pick him at the moment we won't see. But as an ex-Villa man, I hope it's not too long before we do see it."

I suppose Gareth Southgate has a point about the levels of quality expected in the Premier League against the Championship. Snubbing Tottenham before committing to Villa just after the EFL Championship Play-Off Final defeat was a huge gamble for Jack, given his desire to play for England. Villa eventually won the Play-Off Final in May 2019, and Jack had a brilliant 2019 – 2020 season scoring eight goals and provided six assists in the first season back in the Premier League but even that form couldn't convince the England boss to pick Jack, so in a way, it was hard to see what Jack was doing wrong, and hard to see why Gareth wasn't picking him. There was a feeling that Southgate just didn't trust Jack to make that step up or it was 'personal', which I very much doubt myself.

One thing was for sure, Villa fans were getting restless at not seeing Jack in an England shirt.

Regardless to the reasons, it was baffling why he'd been overlooked for so long, being as he had been one of the most consistent performers in both the Championship and the Premier League. Jack's former Villa manager, Tim Sherwood gave some encouragement to Jack in the media and suggested Jack needed to keep his head down and keep working hard, "in the hopes that eventually his time to represent his country will come. Just get back on the football, which is your best friend and hopefully.....it might be injuries that gives him his opportunity and once you get in there, I'm sure when Gareth sees him in close quarters he realises what a talent this boy has."

Sherwood spoke to The Metro a few days before Gareth Southgate was due to announce his squad in august 2020 and ironically, he must have written the script for Jack.

The growing pressure on the England manager ended when Jack's name was finally announced for the two important away fixtures alongside his Aston Villa team-mate, Tyrone Mings. It was the first time he had been included in any England squad since the Under-21 Toulon Tournament in the summer of 2016, ironically, a squad managed by Gareth Southgate himself.

The England manager was left to backtrack on his words slightly a few days after announcing Jack in his squad, because of the injury to Marcus Rashford that ruled him out of the two qualifiers. So, did Southgate call-up Jack to replace him a last-minute thing or would Jack have got the nod if Marcus Rashford had have been fit? That's probably another question entirely.

Although Jack had a stellar season leading up to his inclusion in the squad, Gareth Southgate continued to say that the fierce competition for places kept denying Jack of a place in that England midfield, with regulars Jadon Sancho, Raheem Sterling, Marcus Rashford and Mason Greenwood, as well as the up-and-coming youth players in Phil Foden, Mason Mount, Callum Hudson-Odoi, James Ward-Prowse and James Maddison all vying for forward places. Those names are pretty mouth-watering in their own right, but there are a whole host of talented stars not mentioned, here, Ross Barkley, Alex Oxlade-Chamberlain, Jesse Lingard and the frustrating but talented Dele Alli, who was at one stage a shoo-in for a place in the England line-up. However, it was a mystery to many people, why the England manager included the likes of Sancho, Sterling, Rashford and Greenwood as players competing for the same places as Jack, Foden, Greenwood, Mount, Hudson Odoi and Maddison, as the former players can all be classed as forwards rather than midfielders. To me, they should not be in the same list as Jack.

Southgate also explained that Jack was "unlucky" not to be included in his squads previously but he made an incredible statement when he said he wanted to play Jack in a different role to the one he plays week in, week out for Villa, "We have incredible players in those positions, we have got competition for places. Those four have either been with us for a long time and been exceptional in their performances for us, in terms of Marcus and Raheem." There's no denying those players I've mentioned previously are very good forwards who have been consistently good for England. However, Southgate went on, "I know Villa play Jack as a midfield player (a number 8) – that is not as I see him in the way we play. So, with us he would be a wide player or a number 10, and at the moment I think we have got players who deserve to be in just ahead of him."

Southgate also insisted that Jack was a winger and not a midfielder.

I'm not a football manager, and this is no criticism of Gareth, who I like very much and hold in very high regard, but in my opinion he has been misguided in his description of the way Jack plays. Those comments made to the media just before the squad was announced on 31st August left me scratching my head somewhat, but I'm not the England manager and he's entitled to his opinion, just as anyone else is.

For me, I don't think it's fair on Jack to be included in a pack of four talented 'wide forwards' or 'advanced forwards', whatever you want to call them, who score a Premier League goal on average, every 137 minutes. Those figures are exceptional, and some out-and-out strikers would do anything for those figures. On the other hand, Jack scored a goal every 404 minutes in the 2019 – 2020 season for Villa. It's not fair for Jack to try and emulate the skill of scoring of those England regulars.

Jack's role for Villa has been to come into midfield, get the ball and to run with it at defenders, lay off a pass or two and if he can see an opening, he'll aim at goal. His game isn't to run without the ball and spring offside traps like 'forwards' do. However, one point that many people fail to notice is, although Jack is competing against very different types of players for England, I feel that he has an advantage in that he is 'unique' because there aren't any other players quite like Jack Grealish around, in the way he plays and competes. I'll explain that in due course.

I think the expectation was for Jack to play for England wide on the left of a high-pressing 4-3-3 formation alongside Harry Kane and probably Raheem Sterling, a formation which has become the 'England DNA'. Jack played mostly for Villa in a 'number 8' role; he started the 2019 – 2020 season in that role but was switched to wide left when Villa were left wanting in midfield during that first season back in the Premier League. That sometimes works in Villa's favour because it leaves Jack closer to the opposition goal and it utilises his unique dribbling ability when he carries the ball into space and escapes trouble. Jack is the type of player who attracts people around him, which in turn frees space for other forward players, and you have seen that a lot if you have watched Villa play in the last few years.

Dean Smith first used Jack in a 'number 10' role, out on the left, which effectively saw him move further up the field in a front three for the game at Norwich in October 2019 and it paid dividends straight away when the visitors scored five goals, with Jack scoring the third and was involved in all five. Ok, the Norwich defence were frail, but the 'new' role gave Jack the freedom to dictate play from anywhere on the pitch and he was awesome that day. That move could only have made England manager Gareth Southgate sit up and take note and think that's the position for Jack in his team. However, with the up-coming international games against the Czech Republic and Bulgaria, Jack wasn't thinking of being selected for the squad, "No, not at the moment. I know for a fact if I play to the best of my ability then I can get in there. This time, truthfully, I did not expect to get in. If I keep on performing the way I know I can, hopefully this will give me a big lift and hopefully I will get in soon."

It has been said that Jack apparently doesn't favour that position (the wide left role) and has said he's a 'number 8' but will play a 'number 10' role if asked to do so. On that showing, against Norwich, it's hard to see why he doesn't like the role. Although as the ultimate professional he is, he probably wouldn't complain as long as he's in the team for Villa or for England. Speaking to the media after that performance at Carrow Road, Jack said, "When the manager first pulled me up and asked how I felt about playing there, I said, 'listen, I will play wherever'. Obviously I have my certain positions but I am just happy to be on the pitch. I am captain and I want to lead by example and anywhere I play will be fine. I like this position because I am not really playing as a left winger. I am in off the left, kind of like a number 10."

Like it or not, Gareth Southgate has got a 'unique' player who has the technical ability to lead by example, rather like David Beckham did in his prime; he keeps the ball in tight spaces and maintains patience until he spots an opening. During the 2019 – 2020 season Jack created the second most chances from open play of anyone in the Premier League (75), and only Kevin De Bruyne created more.

In short, Jack is not a Sancho, a Sterling, a Greenwood or a Rashford; Jack's not even similar to most of the other players he's competing with – he's different and that should mean that Southgate can afford to experiment with Jack in the England midfield.

Speaking to Four-Four-Two magazine, the England manager gave a good insight into the way he thinks and perceives players and where they are in his thoughts for selection, and what's behind the reasoning to include Jack or not. Not only did Southgate state the reasons why he saw Jack's role for his country being different to the role he plays for Villa, he stated that the off-field behaviour of his players has a factor in his selections, "The responsibility of being an England player carries a lot of weight. When you're going towards a tournament, you want as little noise as possible around the group. You want the country to connect with the team. You want the country to feel excited and also proud of the team. Also, they must be good ambassadors for everything. On-field decision-making can be reflected in some off-field decision-making. I'm not going to say, 'This is the line and anybody that crosses it we don't consider' because there are so many nuances to it, having to deal with different issues, but we're always observing how players are looking after themselves, how professional they are, how will they be if they're away with us for 35, 40 days next summer? All of these things have to come into our thinking when you're taking a squad away."

Clearly, Southgate had a question mark on whether Jack had the right attitude and mentality in the past to stay in tune with the harmony that has been created in the England camp. A culture that Southgate has created himself, and one which he thinks is the secret to a winning football team. With that in mind, Jack's off-field issues during the COVID-19 lockdown in the spring of 2020 were well documented and couldn't have helped his cause, but he's not the only England player to have had off-field issues. Phil Foden and Mason Greenwood faced their own disciplinary issues, having been sent home after breaching COVID rules during England get togethers.

So, with all that out of the way, at last Jack could look forward to playing his first senior game for England, as he told The Sun, "I don't want to be on the outside looking in again. But I know for that to be the case I've got to make a good impression. It's been a long time coming but this is something I always wanted to do."

There was widespread praise for Jack's inclusion in the England squad for the first time. Former Chelsea. Arsenal and England legend, and some would say 'maverick', Alan Hudson, suggested in the Telegraph that Gareth Southgate should "give him the number 10 shirt and build a team around Jack, because he's that good". Hudson was what could be described as a flair player in the 1970s. He isn't normally so complementary about modern day footballers, but he banged on about Jack, saying he was "the best thing English football has had going for it for a very long time. Certainly, the best midfielder the country has produced since Paul Gascoigne. He is different in every aspect from anyone we have seen lately. For me he could be better than Frank Lampard or Steven Gerard – at international level, that is, for he was born for that stage."

Hudson played during an era of England 'mavericks', Frank Worthington, Stan Bowles, Rodney Marsh, Tony Currie and Peter Osgood, all players who were easy on the eye and played with no fear. His fear for Jack is that he sees history repeating itself, in that the England managers of the 1970s, Don Revie being one, routinely ignored the 'mavericks'. I'm not sure I agree, but I understand his point. For Hudson to see Jack as a kind of 'maverick' player is quite a statement - not that Jack is a 'maverick' in the mould of the aforementioned, but more he's not a 'manufactured' player, but can be seen as 'individual'. Hudson also sees too many modern-day footballers as being like 'robots' and that's probably why he likes Jack. Comparing Jack to Andrea Pirlo and David Silva is probably the best compliment Hudson could give Jack, both uncomplicated, sublime players in their own right and players who go out and play their own game, "Just tell him to go out there and play his game", he said. Hudson went on and said if Jack was Italian, Spanish or French, he would be the first name on the team sheet.

With the 2019 – 2020 season delayed due to the COVID-19 pandemic and eventually ending on 26th July 2020, the players were lacking match practice coming into the two important Nations League internationals with Iceland and Denmark.

Jack was made to wait for his first England debut as he didn't feature in the Nations League fixture in Iceland on 5th September and was named on the bench as an unused substitute, where a

Raheem Sterling penalty late on in stoppage time won it for the Three Lions. Mason Greenwood and Phil Foden made their debuts, Foden coming on for Danny Ings and James Ward-Prowse made his first start in a white shirt.

A few days later, Jack was named on the bench again for the Nations League game in Copenhagen against Denmark, but this time, he finally made his long-awaited bow as a 76th minute substitute for Leeds United midfielder, Kalvin Phillips. It was an uninspiring game and Jack's 15 minutes showed promise, if nothing else.

It was a start, anyway, even though some said it was merely a 'trial' for Jack.

With the 2020 – 2021 season starting over a month later than usual, Gareth Southgate's team checked up on Jack, with Southgate himself attending Villa's opening game of the season against Sheffield United at Villa Park on 21st September and his assistant, Steve Holland watched Jack in the away game at Fulham seven days later. They couldn't have picked two better games to assess Jack as Villa won both games and were very impressive in their 3 – 0 win at Craven Cottage, with Jack getting in on the action with a goal against Fulham. With the upcoming squad announcement for three important (and difficult) internationals in early October, against Wales, Belgium and Denmark Jack poured on the style and gave the England management much food for thought.

Indeed, a few days later Jack was duly named in the England squad for the friendly against Wales and the two incredibly tough Nations' League games. It was a well-timed announcement and went down well with the England fans and the growing number of pundits who had clamoured on the 'Grealish for England' bandwagon. However, the ever-cautious England manager sounded a warning in the pre-match press conference to those same people not to expect too much, too soon from Jack, "For a player like Jack to flourish, there's what he individually can bring, but also then people have got to recognise the moments to be able to give him the ball, the areas of the pitch to be able to give him the ball, the runs to make for him to be able to provide the passes. That's going to be harder to have an immediate impact for him than it would be with his club, where he's playing with those players all the time. We recognise that and I don't want to put huge pressure on him because this is the second camp he has had with us. He got the feel of how we work in the last camp and we got him on to the pitch. He'll play minutes in this camp for sure." Southgate was correct in playing down his inclusion, taking the pressure off him, but some may have seen that as negativity. However, more encouraging comments followed in that press conference to announce the squad, "I want him to go and enjoy his football, do what he does with his club and that, I'm sure, will add to the performance of the team."

But that's football I guess, and it's a game of opinions – it was Gareth Southgate's opinion that Jack wasn't ready before the Wales game and no one can change that. However, for Jack it became almost an obsession to play for England, "My main objective for this season is that I just want to get into the England team; I just think about it all the time. There are so many brilliant players in the Premier League at the moment, so many good English players in them attacking areas - I just think about it all the time. I'm just desperate to go to the Euros. I just pray I can carry on performing, carry on impressing the manager and fingers crossed."

Unlike the previous call-up, when Jack was a late replacement for Marcus Rashford, Jack was called-up into the initial squad, and he was desperate to make his mark. After Villa had made a marvellous start to the 2020 – 2021 season, Jack told the London Evening Standard, he thought he could bring an extra spark and a touch of class to the squad, even though he felt a bit starstruck among the England 'elite', "To finally get the call-up, like the proper call-up where you're in from the start, means much more to me than the last one. I feel comfortable there. I feel like I deserve my place. I am playing against these guys week in, week out. Sometimes you can get starstruck, training with the likes of Raheem Sterling and Harry Kane. They're all human beings at the end of the day and make you feel welcome. This next time I'll be fine because I feel like I deserve to be there. Once you get to know the lads and you speak to them, and you're around them day to day, you realise they're all human. I bring something different to what the other players do and, fingers crossed, I can have a chance … If not this camp then hopefully the next one. That is what I want, I want the chance to show the manager what I can do. I can be that player [who can change a game]. There are people in the team that can do that, look at Ross Barkley, James Maddison... they could. I could as well. There is so much talent in there; [Jadon] Sancho, Sterling. Sometimes it is just tough for the England team because there is a lot of pressure and expectation but I wouldn't mind that, that is what comes being footballers and playing for the national team."

Come the friendly game with Wales, Jack made his first start in an England shirt and he didn't disappoint. In an unfamiliar and experimental line-up, Jack ran the midfield with a swagger. It was very much a second-string side, with Jack playing behind Dominic Calvert-Lewin, on his debut, and alongside Danny Ings in a very experimental 3-4-2-1 formation. Jack was in the action in the 26th minute when he delivered a brilliant cross from the right and the ball landed on the head of the Everton frontman, who was scoring goals for fun at the start of the season.

England's second goal also involved Jack, who looked as if he belonged in the England midfield and had been playing there all of his career. Shortly after the break, Jack drew a foul and a Trippier free-kick was turned in by Conor Coady. Jack was giving a top-class performance and was running the midfield, creating opportunities and drawing fouls in dangerous positions, just like he does, week in, week out for Villa. The performance would have delighted Southgate and the millions of Villa fans watching at home. England subsequently increased their lead in the 63rd minute through a spectacular Danny Ings overhead kick. With the score at 3 – 0, Jack was replaced by Ashley Barnes in the 76th minutes, but did enough to get the Man of the Match award, and deservedly so.

Even if it was only a friendly, if you can call England vs Wales a 'friendly', it demonstrated to everyone watching that the midfield 'maverick' has an important part to play for England, especially with the re-scheduled Euros approaching in the summer of 2021. Gareth Southgate may have finally bowed to media and fan pressure to select him, but for once, that pressure was justified because Jack was worth the adulation.

After the Wales game, Gareth Southgate congratulated Jack for making his debut, "He said, 'well done' and said I've obviously done well in training and he said he'd speak to me soon. I think once you're in the squad they keep in contact with you a bit more." He also told AVTV that Dean Smith texted him after his debut and told Jack how proud he was of him and how much he deserved his chance.

If Jack hadn't have played in the game, it would have been a pretty poor performance but that bit of magic made the difference and he took it upon himself to move around the pitch in order to make something happen. In the absence of Sterling, Sancho and Rashford, Jack was the difference. Not only did he change the course of the game, through unlocking the Welsh defence and drawing fouls in important areas, he assisted the forwards with mouth-watering balls into the box and set-plays.

Some people have an impression of Jack as being a 'luxury player', which is an unfair statement because he showed throughout the Wales game that he isn't averse to tracking back and helping out the defence. It is an area of his game that had improved over the previous 12 months and was evident during Villa's destruction of Liverpool a few days earlier. Also noticeable were his socks, which were rolled down his legs, but maybe not as much as normal, and he played with heavy strapping around his left leg.

After waiting five long years for that chance, Jack took it with open arms and didn't look nervous or shy on the hallowed turf of Wembley. He displayed his usual swagger and confidence, and dropped deep when needed, took the ball when under pressure and switched the play from left to right across the three-man defence.

It is also evident that Gareth Southgate has built his England side around the likes of Harry Kane, Raheem Sterling and Marcus Rashford, and built a 4-3-3 system capable of beating anyone, and why wouldn't he, but on that performance, Jack has given him another option, one he didn't have before the Wales game.

While Villa fans have been trying to convince the rest of the country the virtues of Jack Grealish, that he has been the real deal for several years, Gareth Southgate was left wanting more after the game, speaking about the torment Jack caused on the Welsh defence, saying, "In those deeper areas, he is confident enough to play and you are not thinking he's the type of player who is going to lose the ball in that situation."

The winning of free-kicks in the opposition area is a part of play that England lack, and Jack provided that in abundance. It is now something that Gareth Southgate has in his locker. Getting kicked by the opposition is part of his game and he seems to love it. It seemed from the post-match press conference, Gareth Southgate was impressed with the way Jack handled the multiple kicks he receives during each and every game, "He's a matador in those situations isn't he? The only thing that worries me occasionally is that when he does hang on to the ball, he gets clobbered, and you don't want him to pick up injuries." Every Villa fan worries about the probability of Jack getting injured because of the way he plays, a real-life matador lives for the danger of being attacked by the bull, Jack feeds off the fouls and the niggles that come his way.

While we don't know what is said behind closed doors in the England camp, it has been clear there has been some sort of hesitancy from the England management about selecting Jack, and then slotting him into a system he is comfortable with. As previously stated, Southgate has been quoted as saying Jack is behind Sterling, Rashford and Sancho for a place on the flanks and claiming he could not play as a number 8 or 10 for England. However, after his superb full debut, Jack made it clear that Gareth Southgate is open-minded and good for a chat, "He lets you speak to him and lets you speak your mind, really. I said to him at the time, 'I see myself playing as a number 8 for England. I see myself playing as a number 10. I see myself as a left winger or a right winger. Wherever I am on the pitch, I will play. In the wing positions, there is so much talent. We've probably got the top three or four in the world when you look at Raheem, Marcus and Jadon. It will be difficult to get into these positions. I have full respect for that. But I also have respect for how much ability I have got. I have respect for myself and I know what I can do." Listening to that interview, it says a lot about Jack's confidence in himself and that he doesn't mind the competition in front of him and he seems flexible in where he plays, which is a good thing for a footballer because it shows he's up for the fight and is willing to slot in anywhere for the team.

If the England manager was under extreme pressure to hand Jack his full debut before the Wales game, he was under even more pressure to continue with Jack after it, for the important Nations League game with Belgium a few days later. Maybe Southgate wasn't feeling the pressure, because he decided against picking Jack in the starting line-up, choosing to put him on the bench – and didn't even bring him off it. Mason Mount got the nod in place of Jack, playing alongside Marcus Rashford and just behind Dominic Calvert-Lewis, who was preferred to Harry Kane.

The Villa fans weren't happy with that decision. So, whatever Jack had done in the friendly against Wales seemed to count for nothing when it came to the big game at Wembley against Belgium.

England came from behind to beat Belgium but the fans and pundits who had clamoured for Jack's inclusion for the previous five years were left scratching their heads once again at the manager's team selection as Jack spent the 90 minutes sitting on the bench. They must have been thinking, "Just what has Jack got to do to grab Southgate's attention?"

A few days after the Belgium game, Jack was again omitted from the starting line-up at Wembley, where England had a nightmare, losing Harry Maguire and Reece James to red cards as well as losing the game 1 – 0 to Denmark. Again, he spent the 90 minutes being a spectator, viewing the game from the bench. The worrying thing as a fan was that England didn't create any clear-cut chances, which is why omitting Jack from the game was a mystery. If anyone can create that 'something' it's Jack but try telling that to Gareth Southgate. England sorely lacked creativity during the Denmark game and the manager's decision to leave him out wouldn't have gone down well with the England faithful, nor the frustrated Villa fans.

Fortunately, it wasn't long to wait for the next international break.

Whether or not Gareth Southgate was aware of the increased pressure on him to pick Jack for a competitive start, the England manager was aware of the competition for places between Jack and Mason Mount, who seemed to be winning Southgate's heart, even though Jack was playing well for Villa. However, Jack was included in the squad for the friendly against Ireland at Wembley on 12th November. Southgate joked, and may have wound up the Villa fans at the pre-match press conference, "I suppose on that you're referring to Mason, whose only crime is not to be Jack at the moment. I'm also aware I should talk about Mason because then it keeps the memes going of me talking about Mason. So, we have got to fulfil all those requirements just to keep the Villa fans happy, especially. What would they be able to do on social media if they didn't have that opportunity? So, yes, of course I'm aware Jack's playing well."

It's often been suggested that past England managers have been averse to picking good players, but Southgate insisted his management team weren't "blind to a good player" in the form of Jack Grealish. In the same press conference, Southgate suggested he had found a solution. That solution was to play BOTH Jack and Mason Mount in the friendly against Ireland, two players who had supposedly been in competition for the same place. Mason Mount is obviously a talented player, no doubt, and is four years younger than Jack, so to suggest he was going to include them both in the same side was progress indeed. Mount was assumingly going to play a slightly different role in the centre of midfield, a position England have been short of options for a while.

However, if the question was, if Jack played another man-of-the-match performance against Ireland, will it be enough to convince Southgate to start in the next competitive game? That was a serious debate that was running at the time, serious given the perceived lack of creativity in midfield during the previous competitive game against Denmark – it cried out for a player with the skillset of a Jack Grealish.

For Jack, it was always going to be a special game, being involved in an England squad playing Ireland, the country he represented up until the Under-21s. It was up to Jack to convince his manager he was worthy of a place in the team for the upcoming Nations League games against Belgium and Iceland.

The England manager made suggestion to the challenges he had set Jack, and that was to improve certain parts of his game while playing for Villa, namely creating chances and scoring more goals. Southgate referred to the fact that he had scored a few goals earlier in the season and had several clear-cut chances during recent games, mainly off-the-line clearances in games against Leeds and Arsenal. He also openly challenged Jack to create more chances, "I think we've challenged him on a couple of parts of his game and his response to that has been brilliant. I still think that some of the other players we're talking about are very good players as well and I think it's a shame that, Mason in particular, there seems criticism of him at his club (Chelsea) as well in a similar way."

It was around this time that yet another superstar in the making was just starting to push into the England fold. Jude Bellingham was a little-known attacking midfielder who had made his name playing for Birmingham City, before moving to German club, Borussia Dortmund. He was another player Gareth Southgate knew about, having come through the ranks at Under-15, Under-16, Under-17 and Under-21 level. Bellingham's inclusion into the full England squad for the friendly against Ireland had raised eyebrows, probably because he was vying for the same place as both Mason Mount and Jack Grealish. However, Bellingham had the advantage over Jack that he was playing in the Champions League for Dortmund and Southgate's response to that was, "We could flippantly say, 'well, he's playing for a massive club and he's playing Champion's League football', but there's actually a bit more to it than that. Positionally, he's playing in a two-man midfield for Dortmund, whether that's a 4-2-3-1 or a 3-4-3. So, he's in the exact position that we lost a player in Reece James."

So, for the friendly game with Ireland at Wembley on 12th November, Jack made the starting line-up as expected, on the left of a bank of three, alongside Dominic Calvert-Lewin in the middle and Jadon Sancho on the right. It was another experimental side, with a midfield of James, Mount, Winks and Saka in a 3-4-3 formation. Or was it a 5-2-3 formation? Maybe there's a certain calibre of opponents against which you can get away with playing Sancho, Mount, Grealish, Saka and Calvert-Lewin in the same side, all attacking players of high quality, and Ireland proved to be just that type of opponent.

After the horror show against Denmark, this was a chance to redeem themselves, and they did just that, with Jack running the show once more. He was impressive during his 61 minutes, replaced by Phil Foden, but by that time England were 3 – 0 up and never looked like conceding a goal.

Even though Ireland were, at best mediocre, Jack demonstrated that he has a role to play in the England team in the long-term. Jack relished the 'roving' role Southgate gave him and was confident enough to create chances, including creating an assist for a goal in the 31st minute. Harry Winks worked the ball via Jack to Jadon Sancho on the left, and he cut onto his right foot and shot through the 'keeper's legs, across goal and in at the far post to make it 2 – 0. Jack was happy with his performance, "It was obviously good to get my second start, and I thought we controlled the game well and it's always nice to get the win. I've been trying to score more, assist more this season. I got the assist for Jadon, which I'm happy about, but I could have scored and I could have assisted more. Coming here and training with these guys, it just steps up everything about your game. I'm trying to take as much as I can off them and I think it's helped me."

There was plenty for the England manager to think about after such an inspirational performance by Jack, whose 61 minutes of driving excellence were enough to earn him another man-of-the-match performance and further fired the clamour for his inclusion in a competitive match, of which there were two in quick succession. Southgate commented on Jack's game, "Jadon and Jack, they've got the freedom to go either side of the pitch and create overloads, and I thought at times both of them did that really well. Jack Grealish was very good. He's in really good form and he's playing in the areas we want him to play, not coming too deep, and he's affecting the game in the final third."

Three days after the Ireland game and the optimism gained from the performance, it seemed like England had learned nothing when they travelled to Belgium for another Nations League tie. Ok, they were the top ranked side in the world at the time, but the performance was spineless and they were undone by two early goals. England were without Raheem Sterling so Jack was given his first competitive start and he didn't disappoint. He was the bright spark and the outstanding performer in another poor away display, one which cost their place in the Nations League finals. Jack must have been satisfied with his own display and he did his chances of convincing Gareth Southgate of his pedigree at that level no harm whatsoever, but it also gave the manager a selection headache next time his faithful trio of Sterling, Kane and Rashford were all fit; however, he would have known he could rely on Jack to give him options in the future.

For the third time in three games, Jack had picked up the man-of-the-match award and Gareth Southgate heaped huge praise on him, who this time, trusted him to play for the whole 90 minutes, that's how good he was, and that can only have been good for Jack, letting the world know how much he was warming to seeing Jack play in an England shirt, "We had a different profile of players but in those positions, I thought Jack Grealish had an absolutely outstanding game. Losing Raheem Sterling and Marcus Rashford, we lost a lot of speed. But I can't fault the attacking play until the last chance. I saw somebody (Jack) with the bravery to play, which I knew I would. He took the ball in tight areas, his technique was good, he took players out of the game; and we knew he would buy a lot of free-kicks. I just thought he was outstanding. He should be absolutely delighted with the way he played."

Even captain Harry Kane heaped praise on Jack and said he enjoyed playing with him, as he told The Guardian, "Mase and Jack are really good on the ball, turning defenders and playing one-twos on the edge of the box. I really like playing with Jack – you can see his quality on the ball, one against one, and he's always looking for a forward pass which is great for a striker."

There were plenty of things for Gareth Southgate to think about after that performance, more questions than anything else, not least whether he can fit Jack into the same side as Kane, Sterling and Rashford. Watching that game, I thought Jack had proved he can be the creative player in the side and maybe Southgate will trust him fully by picking him for the Euros starting in June 2021.

One thing was certain, Jack turned Southgate's doubts about him around by 180 degrees.

Next up was another competitive game for England, this time a home game against Iceland on the 18th November. Even though they had failed to qualify for the Nations League finals, Southgate fielded another side which had a mixture of youth and experience, including another start for Jack. This time he featured alongside Phil Foden in a 3-4-2-1 formation, with Harry Kane up top and a midfield of Trippier, Rice, Mount and Saka. Moreover, it was a chance to see the interplay between Harry Kane and Jack in particular. Southgate heaped more praise on the midfielder and he told the pre-match press conference, "Jack Grealish thrives under pressure and can handle the expectation on him. He has had a super start to his international career; I think he will be able to handle the attention."

The game ended in an easy victory for England, 4 – 0, and Jack was superb yet again, and it was a toss-up between Phil Foden, who grabbed himself two goals, and Jack for the award. Jack played his usual attacking game and found himself on the wrong end of never-ending fouls by the Icelandic players, who clearly couldn't keep up with play. Jack lasted 76 minutes, giving way to Jadon Sancho but by then the game was already won.

There was a break between the Iceland game and the next set of internationals in March 2021, three World Cup 2022 qualifiers. Unfortunately, Jack incurred a shin injury while training with Villa in February, so he wasn't available for selection for the three important games.

Speaking after the last international of 2020, Villa manager Dean Smith spoke about Jack and how proud he was that he'd broken into the England team and had proved to everyone he was a top-class player, "I think he has got better gradually. He has always been a top player but he wasn't producing the goals and assists of an attacking midfielder. He started the season really well. He takes things on board. He's clever and asks questions on how he can improve. I am really proud. I have played a full part in his development, gave him the captaincy and seen him grow. Lots of people at Aston Villa have helped nurture him and they will be equally as proud as I am."

Jack spoke to Matt Maher from the Express & Star in February 2021 and gave an insight into how he ticks and his eagerness to improve all the time, "It's definitely helped bring my game on. Watching those players train (in the England camp) and taking little bits from their game. Sometimes it is just speaking to them. It is nice to speak to these people about how they see the game, how they train at different clubs, different cultures. You learn stuff from all these guys, and I feel that is one thing which has helped me massively. As soon as you start playing for the national team, you up your own game. Hopefully there is more to come but as I've said to a lot of people, there is so much talent in the England team in my position. I have to keep doing what I have been doing, keep trying to impress the manager and fingers crossed."

Jack has made such a big impact playing for England he is almost un-droppable, even though Gareth Southgate may not think the same, as there's an abundance of talent waiting to pounce. Speaking to AVTV about his five England appearances, Jack was philosophical about his performances and his need for that elusive first goal, "That's the main thing I want. I've played five games and still yet to score. I knew if I get my chance I could thrive on the biggest stage. For me, playing with these players, training with them, the likes of Harry Kane, Raheem Sterling, I knew if I got the chance to link up with them then I could play the way I have been – I've no doubts about that in my mind. All I've got to do from now on until the end of the season is to play well for Aston Villa, hopefully get more goals, more assists and of course shooting Villa up the table, and come the end of the season, I'm in there for show."

After five games, it seemed like Jack had been in the England squad for years. It must be fairly difficult to adapt from life at your club to the international setup, although these days, most players know each other. Asked how he has adapted to that transition, Jack told AVTV, "When I go away I just try and speak to everyone, especially the more experienced players, and take little ideas off them, like when I'm sitting at the dinner table, I try and sit with different people. Obviously my best mate was Ben Chilwell, who I've known for years. There was one night we were having food and I just stayed and chatted with Jordan Henderson for about an hour after; just asking him questions about his career, which is nice. Obviously, the best thing about going there is training and playing with them, the likes of Harry Kane, especially. The last camp if you'd seen it I probably passed to him a bit too much, because that's what you try and do, give the ball to the best players. He was one who stuck out in my mind who was just out of this world, the way he trains, the way he plays and I think we've all seen that in the Premier League."

While Jack's domestic game improved during the 2020 – 2021 season with Villa, another key development was his breakthrough into the national side and Jack makes no secret of his desire to be in that squad when it's announced by Gareth Southgate. He is "praying to God" that he gets into the England squad as he has "enjoyed every minute (with England) so far."

One day after the squad announcement, the England players were soon back to business with two back-to-back warm-up games at the Riverside Stadium, prior to the Euros finally getting underway.

Gareth Southgate fielded a somewhat experimental side in the first warm-up game against Austria, mainly due to the fact that players from the three teams who'd played in the European finals a few days previously, were excluded. However, there was a starting place for Jack, and he produced the type of performance he would have wanted to produce as he re-established his England credentials following his shin injury.

Jack produced another 'X-Factor' performance, and made things happen in a dull game, with his willingness to run at defences, create space for others and draw fouls in dangerous positions. Basically, he played like he does in every game. He'd done enough and played a big part in the winning goal scored by Bukayo Saka. Jack lasted 71 minutes before being taken off and replaced by Ben White, but it was enough to earn him another man-of-the-match award and a standing ovation from the England fans. However, it appeared he'd injured his shin as he was pictured resting it in an icepack after he returned to the bench, but it was just a precaution.

Gareth Southgate played down injury concerns over Jack, "With Jack, we just felt that that was enough time. I think you can see still a little bit of sharpness still coming and we didn't want to overplay him through that period."

In the second game at the Riverside, this time against Romania, who hadn't qualified for the Euros, Southgate fielded another experimental line-up, but again included Jack in the starting side. It was another dull affair, but it came to life in the 68th minute when Jack ran through the Romania defence and was pulled down in the box by Tiberiu Capusa and the referee gave a penalty, which was converted by Marcus Rashford.

Jack produced another excellent performance and made a big impact, and once again he was man-of-the-match. This time, he lasted the full 90 minutes as England held on for the 1 – 0 win.

With the friendlies out of the way, all Jack was waiting for was to be given the 'nod' from Gareth Southgate to continue his footballing apprenticeship and be picked for Euro 2020.

Chapter 14

ENGLAND'S NEW NUMBER 7 - JACK'S EURO JOURNEY

Jack has some big boots to fill.

The build-up to Euro 2020 started on 1st June 2021 when Gareth Southgate's England squad was announced.

All the talk was whether Jack Grealish would make the 26 or not, especially after his injury which side-lined him for a dozen games.

After a few weeks following the end of the 2020 – 2021 Premier League season, a season like no other, Jack was waiting with bated breath for his name to be called out at Gareth Southgate's squad announcement press conference at St Georges Park. After naming an extended squad a week or so before, the England manager needed to whittle the numbers down from 33 to 26 to take to the tournament held in France, even though most of England's group games were to be played at Wembley.

Jack needn't have worried, because his name was on the list.

What was all the fuss about?

In hindsight, the delay to the Euros due to the COVID-19 crisis actually helped Jack in that, if the championships had gone ahead as scheduled, in June 2020, he most likely wouldn't have made the squad. As the start of the tournament was 12-months behind schedule, that extra time helped Jack's cause. He had a magnificent

2020 – 2021 season with Villa, even considering he had been injured for 11 games during the latter part of the season.

Talking to the Telegraph shortly after the squad was announced, Jack was as excited as a kid in a sweet shop, "I knew that I had the ability and I have had a good season, I am very proud. Gareth briefed us before training this morning (and told us who would be in the 26) so I was buzzing. The first person I told was my mum. I told her that I have got the number seven shirt. I was shocked myself, to be honest. I got told on a WhatsApp, and I got goose bumps. One thing I really like when I come to England is that there is a really good vibe. You have guys that are rivals on a Saturday but when we are here it is like friends getting together. I'd heard 15, 20 years ago that there were groups in the England squad, but really it is not like that now. Gareth really gets us together and we are mates. I have never come here expecting to play, but yeah of course, getting in the XI is my goal. Everyone else in my position seems to have just played in a Champions League or Europa League final so it is difficult. I had a conversation with John McGinn where I said, I dunno, if there's only 10,000 fans maybe it would be better to wait, will you be able to hear a noise? And then we went out for the Villa warm up and I came back and I said Oh bro you were right it was very noisy."

What's more, Jack was handed the famous number '7' shirt, previously held by such players like David Beckham, Bryan Robson, Kevin Keegan. And Alan Ball in 1966.

What more could Jack want? His dream had come true and it was all about to start on 11th June.

In an interview with BBC Sport, Jack said he "would cherish every moment" of Euro 2020 as he prepared for his first major tournament, something he said he wanted his whole life".

After winning seven caps since his first in September 2020, Jack started dreaming about his next step, and that was to break into the first team and contribute to England's push for Euro glory. Jack told BBC Sport, "I remember watching Russia in 2018. It was crazy how football brought the whole nation together. Even my nan who never watches football was watching every game. I remember Euro 2004 when Rooney burst onto the scene. It sticks in the memory. You grow up thinking about these things and dreaming of them. It'll be unbelievable. My family are so excited already. It'll be a great feeling for them to watch me at a major tournament. Hopefully I get on the pitch and express myself at some point and make them proud."

2nd June 2021
First warm-up game

England 1 Austria 0

England's countdown to the Euro's started with a tough game against Austria. After naming his 26-man squad, which included Jack, Gareth Southgate fielded another experimental side against their fellow Euro 2020 finalists at the Riverside Stadium and Jack was included in a 4-2-3-1 formation, which included a midfield of Rice and Bellingham, and forwards Lingard, Grealish and Saka.

It was fitting that Saka scored his first international goal on 56 minutes, illustrating his value to England, while Jack produced another man-of-the-match performance that fully deserved the ovation he received when he came off, replaced by Ben white in the 71st minute.
Jack was England's main creator and driving force, with his manager commenting to the post-match press conference, "Jack Grealish showed some lovely touches. You can see he's still getting to full fitness - with the bursts you know he can make. He's a quality player."

6th June 2021
Second warm-up game

England 1 Romania 0

England concluded their preparations for Euro 2020 with victory over Romania at the Riverside Stadium. Manager Gareth Southgate once again selected an experimental starting line-up which included the three players - Ben Godfrey, Ben White and James Ward-Prowse - who were not named in his 26-man squad for Euro 2020.

Jack was named again, alongside Jaden Sancho and Marcus

Rashford and he continued to make a good case for inclusion in England's starting line-up for the start of the Euros campaign. In a patchy England display, Jack was once again the brightest attacking spark, creating as well as drawing fouls in dangerous positions throughout. It was on another trademark raid into the area that Jack drew the foul that delivered England their match-winning penalty, which was converted by Rashford, giving his team the confidence of a second successive victory.

Jack certainly gave Southgate plenty of food for thought in these two games as he lasted the whole 90 minutes this time. Two man-of-the-match performances clearly demonstrated Jack certainly has the 'X Factor' that can make an impact in major tournaments when his team need it.

Southgate was again pleased with Jack's contribution, saying, ""We have a lot of competition in those areas of the field. He did well to win the penalty."

With the friendlies out of the way, Gareth Southgate and the England squad were looking forward to the start of the tournament. Speaking to the BBC before the kick-off, Southgate said he knew Jack was itching to start, but as we all know, he isn't one to be persuaded by the general opinion or by media pressure to include Jack from the start, "Sterling and Foden provide some continuity from our matches in March. I think they and Kane have an understanding and we have fabulous depth. We know that Marcus Rashford and Jack Grealish are really pushing for starting positions but we're going to need all those players for this game in the heat."

13th June 2021
Group D Game 1

England 1 Croatia 0

Although Gareth Southgate played Jack in the two warm-up games prior to the start of Euro 2020, he resisted the temptation to start him in the opening group game at Wembley in front of 22,500 fans. The England midfield took a familiar 4-3-3 with Phillips, Rice and Mount behind a front three of Foden, Kane and Sterling.

There was criticism of Southgate for the starting selection, with no Jack and no Marcus Rashford in what was seen as a mixture of caution and adventure.

A single goal by Raheem Sterling gave England a narrow but well-deserved opening game victory and more importantly, three points in the locker.

Unfortunately, there was no room for Jack, who was named on the bench and didn't feature in the entire game, even though the Wembley crowd were calling his name just before Sterling scored the only goal. In fact, the crowd booed the decision not to bring Jack on, with the manager choosing to bring on Jude Bellingham.

18th June 2021
Group D Game 2

England 0 Scotland 0

Jack was on the bench again for England's big clash with the Auld enemy, Scotland, in front of 22,500 fans at Wembley. It was the first meeting between the teams in a major tournament since Euro 96 and it was played in a typically raucous and hostile atmosphere.

With the score 0 – 0 and England struggling to get past the resolute Scottish defence, Gareth Southgate answered England's fans' calls and sent on Jack in the 63rd minute, replacing Phil Foden and he instantly won a corner and got his side ticking down the left flank.

Although the game ended goalless, England's go-to man in their crisis of creativity won four fouls during his 27 minutes on the pitch, but he didn't quite live up to the clamour, although he did plenty of good work after his introduction. However, the usual media and fan hype were calling for him to start against Croatia, but that of course was up to the manager.

The England fans wanted to see Jack come on all through the game and halfway through the second half they could be heard singing, "Super, Super Jack...." After his tournament debut, Jack spoke to

BBC Sport and said he was proud to hear his name being sung by the England fans, "It was nice to have them cheering my name – most of the time I'm getting booed by these fans on a Saturday." Jack continued, "I tried to be as fearless as possible, tried to take people on, I felt like I did. The only thing I could have improved on was my final ball. There's only one person who you have to impress and that's the manager. I think everyone knows how much I love playing, and I want to play and hopefully I do get my chance soon."

Jack also spoke how proud his family were when he finally came off the bench, "My mum texted me straight away after the game. I think she was a bit emotional. I feel I can make them even prouder."

The big test will come if and when Jack gets the nod to start the next game, against Czech Republic at Wembley, "It will be one of the proudest moments of my life, wearing that number 7 shirt it will fill me with so much confidence. Pressure is a privilege and that's the way I've always seen it. I'll go out there and play with a smile on my face. That's when I'm happiest, with the ball at my feet."

22nd June 2021
Group D Game 3

Czech Republic 0 England 1

After coming off the bench against Scotland a few days earlier, Jack was indeed named in the starting line-up by Gareth Southgate, to the joy of millions of Villa fans, not to mention tens of millions of England fans.

While it was assumed Jack started at Wembley on merit, Mason Mount's absence was due to him being in 'close contact' with Scotland star, Billy Gilmour after the last group game so he had to go into self-isolation after Gilmour tested positive for COVID.

However, as they say, one person's misfortune is another's opportunity, so Jack, Harry McGuire and Bukayo Saka got their chance to start and give them a freshness they needed after the dour goalless draw against Scotland. The enforced absence of Mount created an opening behind captain Kane and, with Phil Foden left out, it gave a big opportunity for Jack and Bukayo.

Jack was a popular choice with the fans, his name being cheered loudly when it was announced, and he delivered a vibrant first-half performance in which he was a constant threat, demanding the ball and always attempting to pose problems for the Czech defence. And as if he needed anymore inspiration to perform to the best of his ability, it only took him 12 minutes to make a significant contribution in the game. Both him and Saka were two of England's better performers on the night. In a performance that developed into a slog after a bright start, Raheem Sterling converted at the far post in the 12th minute from Jack's inch-perfect cross after fine work from Saka.

Instead of being substituted, Jack lasted the full 90 minutes and came close to being man-of-the-match, with that accolade going to Saka, who was energetic and looked at home on the big stage.

England's second win out of the three group games helped them qualify as group winners with 7 points, with a mouth-watering Round of 16 tie against Germany awaiting them.

29th June 2021
Round of 16

England 2 Germany 0

Jack was on the bench again for the big game with Germany. Southgate has picked a strong line-up and a 3-4-3 formation with Trippier, Phillips, Rice and Shaw in midfield, behind Saka, Kane and Sterling.

The action didn't start until the 69th minute with the score at 0 – 0, the moment the game changed, the moment every Villa and England fan had been waiting for – the arrival of Jack Grealish. I say changed, because Jack really did make an immediate impact.

The team selection raised a few eyebrows when the manager decided to leave the creative talents of Jack and Phil Foden on the bench and showed huge faith in Bukayo Saka by starting him. However, Saka was excellent and so were England, but the arrival of Jack in the 69th minute, who ironically replaced Saka, was significant to say the least. The 40,000 fans inside Wembley jumped for joy when Jack's name was announced as a substitution and it didn't take long for him to get into the action. Six minutes after coming on, Jack linked up with Harry Kane and Luke Shaw for Sterling to steer the ball in to make it 1 – 0. However, the big moment came with the goal that settled the game. There was another moment of brilliance four minutes from time when Harry Kane, who had struggled to find his form in the group games, headed in from Jack's perfect delivery for his first goal of Euro 2020. It was Jack's second assist in two games – and it signalled his arrival onto the international scene with a bang, even though he had been used more as an impact sub.

Jack had contributed to both goals and that is why so many wanted him on the pitch. He provided the pass to set up Shaw's assist for England's opening goal and then delivered the pinpoint cross for Kane to make the game safe. Gareth Southgate would of course argue that the cameo role suits Jack's game, but there is no doubt the manager had his tactics spot on again.

It was 2 – 0 to England, who had defeated Germany in a competitive game at Wembley for the first time since the 1966 World Cup final, having been winless in their previous three such encounters.

7th July 2021
Semi-Final

England 2 Denmark 1
(After Extra-Time)

England's mission was to go one-step further than any other team had done since July 1966 and that was to the final of a major international tournament. In front of 66,000 at Wembley, they finally achieved glory against a tough Denmark side who went in front on the half hour.

Jack was again on the bench, with Mason Mount taking the central midfield role with Saka and Sterling alongside him. With the score at 1 – 1 at half-time, Jack came on to a rapturous ovation on the 69th minute to replace Saka, with the game increasingly looking as though it was going into extra-time. And, so it did, although there was a late flurry of activity, nothing could stop the extra 30 minutes. Gareth Southgate has had to contend with the perception of a manager who is defence-first, and as the clock ticked down, he wanted to protect England's lead first and foremost, so Jack became only the third England player to be substituted as a substitute in a major tournament when Trippier came on in the extra-time half-time break, giving Jack 40 minutes game time.

It was a strange thing to do, subbing a sub, but I think most football people would appreciate Gareth's decision, although it got slammed by some pundits in some quarters of the media.

Although the unofficial 'Jack Grealish Appreciation Society' didn't approve of the manager's decision, it worked wonders as Harry Kane popped up to score the winner in the 109th minute and led England to their first final since 1966.

Jack had played 150 minutes in the tournament so far and made two assists, started once but certainly made an impact from the bench, especially against Germany. Not a bad first tournament for Jack it could be said.

An insight into how Jack and others spent some of their spare time were made in comments to the Birmingham Mail by Phil Foden, "Me and Jack after training just love to spray the balls in the air and keep it up and not let it touch the ground. We try and fit that in after training. The coaches are not too happy, but we always try to do it after training," he added. Maybe the coaches don't appreciate the extra work.

11th July 2021
Final
Italy 1 England 1
(Italy won 3 – 2 on penalties)

Jack was again named as a substitute for the most important game any England side has played in since July 1966. He had a long wait too – right until extra-time in fact, with the scores level at 1 – 1. By that stage the game was locked on course for the dreaded penalty shoot-out. With 30 minutes of extra-time under his belt, Jack didn't really have any opportunity to showcase his talent, with the stubborn, and sometimes aggressive Italian backline dominating proceedings.

Apart from the first-half, it was a poor display by England and the penalty shoot-out was even more so, with only the two Harry's, Kane and McGuire scoring and three of the new breed of talent missing badly. Jack was seen on TV before the shoot-out commenced, offering his services to take a penalty, and in hindsight, if a sixth penalty-taker was required, you'd guess Jack would have been called upon, but it wasn't to be.

The decision to use three of the younger players instead of the likes of Trippier, Walker, Shaw or Jack was criticised in the media and by some fans on social media. Writing on Twitter, Jack said, *"I said I wanted to take one!!!! The gaffer has made so many right decisions through this tournament and he did tonight! But I won't have people say that I didn't want to take a peno when I said I will."*

England's wait for another major trophy goes on, and Qatar awaits the new breed of England players, including Jack who are now more experienced after taking part in a final and taking Italy all the way, but ultimately, not far enough.

As for Jack, he went on holiday following that final, contemplating his future.

Chapter 15

BRITAIN'S FIRST £100M PLAYER

Jack signs for Manchester City for a British transfer record.

On 15th September 2020 Jack Grealish signed a 5-year deal with Aston Villa worth around £125,000 a week, but at the time nobody knew if he would see out the full term. There was talk of a huge buy-out clause being part of the contract, one that protected Villa's interests and one that, at the time, no other club would even contemplate breaking.

Fast-forward 12 months and Jack put pen to paper on a £100m British record transfer to Manchester City, the only club that anyone could reasonably see paying that sort of money for the hottest property on the British football scene.

Jack had been given an extended break from his return to pre-season training with Villa, following his involvement in the England squad during the Euros; he wasn't expected to return to Bodymoor Heath until 2nd August. Up until then, it had been relatively quiet on the rumour front, even though Manchester City had started to come in hard with their opening offer of £100m on 29th July.

Villa's stance had always been one of defiance, that they had no intention to sell their prized asset, and why would they? CEO, Christian Purslow was due to sit down with Jack to discuss a bumper new deal said to be around £200,000 a week and were said to be 'confident' in keeping Jack for the forthcoming season.

Having said all of that, the only person who had a decision to make was Jack Grealish himself, because if he wanted to move, then he would move and no amount of money would change his mind.

What the media and the fans didn't know was, what clauses were in the contract, because at the end of the day, there had to be at least one.

Another important player in the sage was Jack's agent, Jonathan Barnett, who had remained coy all along about whether his client would stay at Villa or leave for a perceived 'bigger club'. Barnett's camp included the likes of Jack's England teammates, Mason Mount, Jordan Pickford, Ben Chilwell and Luke Shaw, all who holidayed with Jack in the summer. With Barnett becoming increasingly vocal about Jack and keen to cash in on his client while his profile and stock was high, it became obvious that something was about to happen.

As for City, their pursuit of a striker was seemingly more important than the purchase of yet another midfielder, but that was becoming more difficult to achieve so their attention began to move to securing the signature of Jack. The amount of stories in the media increased during the latter days of July and into the first few days of August and there was a feeling that negotiations were at an advanced stage, even though there was still a lot of work to be done to secure his signature.

Of course, at that stage, Jack himself hadn't spoken about his future and all the talk was circumstantial at best.

While all the work in the background was going on, Jack had joined his Villa teammates at their pre-season camp in London, ahead of their first game of the season against Watford. He was pictured doing some light training and talking to fans who had turned up to watch the training sessions. Even then, Villa fans still believed their captain was going to stay at Villa, given he had re-joined the rest of the first-team squad, but Jack of course had a different perspective.

On the 4th August, it became clear that Jack's move was indeed going ahead following the departure of City midfielder, Bernardo Silva. It was widely expected that any transfer would be concluded within 48 hours. On that same day, former Villa striker, Stan Collymore claimed he had 'inside information' that the transfer had been completed after Jack had reportedly travelled to Manchester for a medical and to agree personal terms. Collymore's Tweet broke Villa's hearts:

"Deal is done. Signed. Jack Grealish, sincere best wishes, thank you for your efforts."

His comments left Villa fans rightly frustrated at losing their star man and Collymore had sympathy with them, saying:

"Villans are upset because they lived their love of our club through you so it will sting for a while. Villans, forwards."

The lure of Champions League football was too much for Jack Grealish to turn down, but not only that, working with Pep Guardiola, probably the best coach in the world, was equally an incentive for the 25-year-old. If you add to that, the talk from England manager, Gareth Southgate, saying Jack had to play in the Champions League if he wanted to hold his England place, then any hope Villa fans had of him staying at Villa Park were null. It was disappointing for Villa fans, but in the world of modern football, money talks.

However, the proposed move to City didn't seem to be a popular one amongst all their fans. Oasis frontman and City fan, Liam Gallagher Tweeted:

*"100 ******** million pounds. If that's the case, Foden must be worth 500 million plus."*

Indeed, on 6th August the Jack signed for the Premier League Champions for a British transfer record of £100m on a six-year deal for a reportedly £325,000 a week. The move eclipsed the £93.25m transfer of Paul Pogba to Manchester United in 2016. It was eventually made public that City activated a release clause in Jack's 2020 Villa contract that allowed him to join a club in the Champions League once that club had offered £100m.

Pep Guardiola had been a long admirer of Jack and was delighted to have signed him. With the departure of City legend Sergio Aguero, Jack was immediately given his Number 10 shirt. Jack's first comments during his press conference were, "I am incredibly happy to have joined Manchester City. City are the best team in the country with a manager considered to be the best in the world – it's a dream come true to be part of this club. Over the past 10 seasons, they have won major trophies consistently. Pep coming here has taken them to the next level and the football this team plays is the most exciting in Europe. To play for Pep and learn from him is going to be special and it's something any top footballer would want. The facilities are amazing, and I honestly can't wait to get started, meet everyone and get playing."

The guru behind so many top signings, City Director of Football, Txiki Begiristain added, "We are absolutely delighted to be able to welcome Jack Grealish to Manchester City. He is an incredible talent. Jack's development over the past few seasons both for club and country has been plain for everybody to see. His natural talent together with his commitment to improve as a player, has seen him become one of the most exciting attacking players in world football today. I am certain that the fans are going to love seeing him in our team. Pep loves the way he plays, and we all feel he is an ideal fit for Manchester City. Our style and his style are a perfect match. I'm excited to watch him over the coming years."

All of those words from both Jack and Begiristain would have sent shivers down the spines of Villa fans but there was nothing they could have done to have stopped the transfer going ahead. It was clear that there was only one club he was going to sign for.

Jack used his Twitter account to comment on his transfer:

"It was obviously a difficult few months because I have been an Aston Villa fan for my whole life. But when I spoke to the manager here and you see what type of players they have got here, in the end it was something I couldn't say no to."

From a Villa perspective, a refreshingly clear, concise and honest view was outlined by Christian Purslow in a live broadcast on

Villa's TV channel, VillaTV. The Villa CEO explained why the release clause was inserted into the contract in the summer of 2020 and explained that Jack wanted to be notified if a Champions League club activated the £100m figure. He said that a number of clubs expressed an interest in Jack after the Euros but all the offers were well below the release clause figure. The hugely popular Christian Purlslow explained further, "It was a highly emotional moment when he finally told me his decision, leaving me in no doubt how hard it had been for him to leave our club, which he had joined when he was six years old. Ultimately he said it boiled down to wanting to play Champions League football now."

However honest Purslow was during that broadcast, his words wouldn't have sounded any better to the listening Villa fans, who had just lost their best player.

So, where will Jack fit into the City team?

With an abundance of forward-thinking players already at their disposal, Jack only adds more fire-power to the likes of Stirling, Foden, Mahrez, De Bruyne, Gundogan and Torres. City usually play with effectively five forwards so Pep now has one more superstar to use in his rotation system. Imagine a midfield three of: Grealish, Foden and De Bruyne.

Although Villa fans have seen the tantalising talent of Jack Grealish for many years, the question all City fans are interested in is what Jack could do at the top end of the Premier League and in the Champions League. That question can't be answered here, but in another 12 months we will all find out. It seems to me that the signing of Jack is seen as future-proofing the City midfield, given that Gundogan is into his 30s and the 'main man', De Bruyne is over 30. In another 12 to 18 months from the time of writing, Jack may be the 'main man' in that City midfield. It is a trademark of Pep that he plans his teams in 18-month spells and the signing of Jack could be one of those. Having said that, I bet he hopes Jack fits into the team quicker than Mahrez did. His transition from being the 'main man' at Leicester to 'just another attacking midfielder' at City was a struggle. Jack was the 'main man' at Villa, but he won't be that at City – not immediately anyway.

On the Monday after Jack's big day, he was officially unveiled to the City fans and the media at the Ethiad Stadium on a giant platform in front of the Colin Bell Stand. It was evident that Jack is the poster boy of Manchester and he will soon become the marketing man's dream and earn City lots of money.

Jack then gave a press conference and said that the price tag wouldn't have any effect on him or his game and wouldn't add to the pressure put on him, "No it don't put no pressure on me whatsoever. I take that as a compliment. I actually like it. I think it is a good tag to have. I think when you see a club paying that much for a player it means they trust and value you highly and see so much potential there to work with. I just see it as a good thing. Now I just hope I can repay this whole football club by winning as many titles as possible and winning that trophy we all want. I think when you see a club paying that much for a player it means they trust and value you highly and see so much potential there to work with. I just see it as a good thing. Now I just hope I can repay this whole football club by winning as many titles as possible and winning that trophy we all want. It probably hasn't sunk in yet actually. It means so much to me that the club were willing to spend that much money on me. If anything, it just fills me with confidence. I don't think there's any pressure on that price tag at all. It just shows how much the club and the manager value me and that only gives me confidence going forward."

Jack then spoke about leaving Villa, "It's been a crazy few days, something I've never experienced before. I've been at Aston Villa my whole life, it's been different. Going into a new changing room, I've not done that before, I've enjoyed every minute of it. Everyone at the club, backroom staff to players, have made me and my family feel so welcome. It was so tough [to leave Villa], I think everyone knows I reported back for pre-season as I was meant to, I went back for a few days, it was difficult, in the back of my head I knew I might be going. I did a bit on my own, everyone saw how Messi was yesterday (he cried at leaving Barcelona), that's the exact way I felt, before I left at the hotel I spoke to the team and the staff and the players and I teared up a little bit myself."

Jack also indicated that he would become a lesser target for the foulers and players wouldn't gang up on him, like they did when he was a Villa player, and that could spell danger for opponents, "Sometimes at Villa I would get doubled up," he said. "Here it would be more difficult because there's so much talent all over the pitch that it might be harder for teams to double up on me, which will give me more space and freedom to attack players one v one."

Speaking about his excitement of playing in the Champions League, he admitted it was hard watching other teams competing against the likes of Paris St-Germain, Barcelona and Real Madrid, "I remember speaking to John Terry (the former Chelsea captain) at Villa and he said to me when you're standing there and hear that Champions League anthem played there's nothing better," he said. "I can't wait to be doing that. I fully believe we can win it this year."

Of course, another reason why Jack has moved on is because of his chances to play regularly for England under Gareth Southgate. It has been made clear to Jack that he needed to play in the Champions League in order to be a regular and I have mentioned this in previous chapters. My view is that no player has to play in the Champions League in order to play for England; if he's good enough, then he should play for his country. Take Calvin Phillips for example. He's been picked for most England games recently and he doesn't play Champions League football for Leeds, so why should Gareth dangle that carrot in front of Jack? After being used as an impact substitute in the Euros (in 2021), Jack now hopes to be a regular by the time the World Cup finals come along in Qatar in November 2022 and working with Pep will only enhance his chances, especially if City land Harry Kane in the winter transfer window (or in the 2022 summer transfer window). On this point, Jack said, "We're all young and striving for success with our club and the national team. I think that's something the England manager will love really because it gives you that chemistry."

****

Jack's City Debut.

Just one day after signing for City, Jack made his debut in the FA Community Shield at Wembley against FA Cup winners Leicester

City in front of a low crowd of 45, 602. In the 65th minute, coming on as a substitute for City youngster, Samuel Edozie his City career officially began. Given he hadn't had any match practice for several weeks, since the remaining minutes of the Euro 2020 Final, it wasn't surprising Jack couldn't influence the game, particularly with City missing a centre-forward, with Aguero gone and the proposed Harry Kane transfer saga still rumbling along at the time. City lost the game in the 89th minute with a penalty from Iheanacho.

Pep played Jack on the left side of the front three, but it was probably more of an experiment than anything else. His involvement was limited to say the least, apart from one smart dribble and one neat pass inside the box. In fact, he lost possession quite a bit which is something not acceptable to Pep.

Speaking about Jack's 25-minute cameo appearance, Pep said, "He didn't come to play 25 minutes, he came to play five or six years. How can he build a relation when his mates are not here? But it's not a problem, he knows Kyle [Walker] and Raz [Sterling] and Phil [Foden] and John [Stones] they are back tomorrow. We just need to provide him and let him express his quality."

The first Premier League game of the season for City was a trip to the new Tottenham Hotspur Stadium. Even with the absence of Harry Kane from the Spurs starting line-up, and a first start for Jack in his number 10 shirt, Son Heung-min spoilt Jack's day with a 55th minute winner. Spurs were the better side and deserved the win in Nuno Espirito Santo's first game in charge of the Lilywhites. Jack had a surprisingly quiet debut and was shown a yellow card late on for a foul on Lucas Moura. Pep said Jack was "excellent" and maybe he was, making some useful contributions early on, but he also suggested Jack wasn't fit and had a lot of work to do to integrate his talents into the squad.

It really wasn't the start of his Manchester City career Jack was hoping for. Things can only get better.

The first home game saw City back to business as usual with a 5 – 0 win against Premier League new-boys, Norwich City. For Jack, it was party time as he saw his new side demolish Norwich from start to finish. In fact, Jack felt right at home and also got on the scoresheet on the 22nd minute for City's second goal. If the Spurs game was a disaster, this game was the opposite as Jack seemed to click everything into place and integrated himself with his new adoring fans, thanks to his goal and a busy display. Jack lasted 75 minutes before being replaced by Mahrez, but the signs were there that he would make a difference in the City line-up.

Another home game followed, this time against Arsenal, another start for Jack and another 5 – 0 demolition for City. Jack was in the game when he teased up Gabriel Jesus for City's third on the 43rd minute. Again, City went into the game without an orthodox number 9, but on that display, do they need one?

More pleasing for Jack was that he picked up the man-of-the-match award.

****

On England Duty.

On the eve of England's World Cup qualifier against Hungary on 2nd September 2021, Jack did an interview with ITV and it was aired before the game. I bet in hindsight that Jack wished he'd chosen his words more carefully because the output from it stirred up the Villa fans and turned them against their former hero.

Sat in the sports hall at St George's Park, Jack spoke to Gabriel Clarke and appeared to come across in a different light to the innocent 'Super Jack' all Villa fans have come to love. Who was this unrecognisable person Villa fans asked on social media outlets in their thousands? What appeared to be an innocent, open and honest interview with the 'most expensive footballer in Britain' became a war of words, not only with a large proportion of Villa fans, but with a local newspaper journalist.

The Birmingham Mail claimed some of the words in the interview were "painful, and to some extent, insulting words about his boyhood club." One question that hit the wrong note with the Villa faithful, was when Clarke asked if he ever thought the £100m get out clause would be met, to which Jack replied, "Maybe, yeah. That's why we had it put in…" Then there was a pause from Jack, who seems to realise what he'd said may trigger some reaction from certain quarters. In hindsight, he could have been less cold about his answer, an answer that was perceived by some as "lacking total respect to Aston Villa Football Club" (not my words). That one-liner irked and angered Villa fans and they took to social media in their droves. The newspaper article that followed the interview rubbed it in even more, and suggested Jack "may as well have tweeted out, 'My city. My club. My release clause just 12 months ago when he signed his five-year deal to become Villa's highest-paid player in the club's history.'"

The fact that Jack signed that five-year deal in September 2020 and that he believed in the Villa project, suggested he was odds-on to stay with Villa for longer than the 11 months he actually did. However, the vibe the Birmingham Mail took from that statement suggested, "I couldn't wait to get out", but personally, I doubt that was on Jack's mind – how could he think like that, given he is a life-long Villa fan who has captained his club?

Another suggestion from Jack was that the move would give his England chances a big lift and was a "massive reason" behind the transfer, something I have spoken about before, "I feel to be playing for England in the biggest of games I need to be playing at club level in the biggest of games, that'll be the Champions League, all these types of games." The Birmingham Mail made the comparison with the Calvin Phillips, Jordan Pickford and Declan Rice situation, all who have never played in the Champions League and stirred the pot with that one, with the comment, "Come off it, Jack."

However, the answer Jack gave to one question left Villa fans a gasp. After less than a month at the Ethiad, Clarke asked Jack if he was a better player and his reply was, "Yeah, 100 per cent. You just pick up stuff from certain players. Everyone's an international at a top, top country. It makes you up your standards." The Birmingham Mail ended the article with, "Now that's not much of an endorsement for his former teammates at Villa, is it?" It went on, "There was just zero affection for Villa, a club he banged on about loving, in Grealish's first England interview since leaving. It just stank of 'Villa aren't good enough for me, I'm better than that.'"

Looking at the interview, I think Jack was less than conciliatory with his words, but I don't really think he meant it in the way the Birmingham Mail made the interview out to be, although he probably could have been a bit less cold in his choice of words. All-in-all, the interview, the body language and the choice of words were a shocker. Whether Jack "lacked class" as the Birmingham Mail suggested is another matter, but it was cringe-worthy TV viewing all the same – for Villa fans, anyway.

Whatever the intentions of the interview, it certainly rattled a few feathers but the reaction from the Birmingham Mail article also irked Jack as he replied to the same journalist on Twitter and got himself into a spat with him:

"This is the worst and most one-sided article I've ever seen... Classless? Jealous? Couldn't wait to get out? Arrogance? How exactly? I've been a Villa fan my whole life and still am. The thing is you don't understand what goes on in the real football world."

Advantage Jack I'd say. That was really a comeback.

Now to the football. It was no surprise really that Jack made the starting line-up for England's World Cup qualifier away to Hungary. In a very intimidating atmosphere in Budapest, the England lads did themselves proud with a thoroughly professional performance and a convincing 4 – 0 win. Gareth would have been delighted with jack's performance, linking up well with Mason Mount and Declan Rice, although it was Kalvin Phillips who grabbed the headlines with a man-of-the-match performance, although Jack was a close second.

Jack's major contribution came in the 87th minute, with an assist to Declan Rice's goal, England's fourth.

Three days later, England were back at Wembley to face Andorra. It was all-change again for England, and Jack, along with many of the other big names, found themselves on the bench, to give the 'fringe' players a runout. Jack got his chance in the 62nd minute with the score 1 -0 and it seemed that there needed to be an injection of something to spark the game into life. On comes Jack, along with Mount and Harry Kane. Boom! Three goals in the final 30 minutes were enough to see off Andorra.

The final game of the triple-header came in Poland. The big players were back for this tough game and that included Jack. Although a Harry Kane wonder-strike settled the England nerves in the 72nd minute, Jack wasn't at his usual best, as he found it frustrating to get hold of the ball in front of another Partizan home crowd. Although England controlled the game, disappointment came in the third minute of injury time when a lack of concentration in the England box saw Poland equalise. For the second game in three, Kalvin Phillips was man-of-the-match, with Jack a close second yet again.

At the time of writing, it is a pivotal moment in the career of Jack Grealish, both for his new club and for England, where he will be viewed in a different light by Gareth Southgate, who will be dealing with a player who plays in the Champions League.

The world will be waiting to see what unfolds for Jack Grealish – Britain's First £100m Player.

EPILOGUE

It has taken a while, but Jack Grealish has become the complete footballer everyone thought he would and has become an important part of the England national team.

There's so much more to Jack Grealish than just the footballer player. From my own observations going back six or seven years, watching this raw young talent with a silky-smooth style and undoubted natural ability appear on the scene, to watching the Jack Grealish of 2021, captain of Aston Villa FC, an England international and now part of Pep's Manchester City machine has been a complete revelation.

Well done Jack! You have proved all of your doubters wrong; people who, only a few years ago, doubted his undisputed talent would ever make it in the big time, and doubted he would convince Gareth Southgate he was worthy of wearing the England shirt. In my opinion, England now have a player who can grace the Wembley pitch for many years to come.

Researching this book has opened my eyes to the fact that Jack Grealish is not only a sensational footballer, probably the best English footballer I've seen since Paul Gascoigne, but he's also a fascinating character, a very charitable guy and someone who knows exactly what he wants - and what he wants is to be the best footballer in the Premier League.

As a lifelong Aston Villa and England fan, I can only watch from the stands or from my armchair (during COVID) and watch a footballer who gets people off their seats; he gets me off my seat that's for sure, and you can't say that about too many 'manufactured' and average footballers these days. Having said that, England has produced, and is producing some brilliant young talent over the last five or six years, with the help of Gareth Southgate, the England manager, bringing youth to the forefront and giving them the chance to shine. The likes of Kane, Sterling, Sancho, Rashford, Maddison, and the list goes on. Add the name of Jack Grealish and it's a mouth-watering list.

Going back to our Jack, he's a unique talent; there is no other player I can think of who plays like he does for club and country. Players simply can't read his game and all they have in their locker is to foul him, deck him and to try and get him to react. Going back a few years, Jack used to react, and it got him in the referee's book a fair few times, but now, he brushes off the tackles, dusts himself down, smiles and gets on with the play – there is rarely any reaction to the foulers in the game. That part of his game has improved 100 times and it's all down to him enjoying his football and how he's learned to react to incidents.

It can be said that his football career has not been an easy passage and has taken many twists and turns but every step of the way, it seems that Jack has relished the challenge and ultimately won against the odds.

Being made captain by Dean Smith was the making of Jack Grealish, not only as a footballer, but as a person, that is for sure. It was probably a gamble by Smith; he must have known what he was doing, or maybe it was just pure luck, because with Jack as captain, Villa went on to win 10 straight games and qualified for the Championship play-offs, and ultimately won promotion.

Since that great day at Wembley in late May 2019, Jack's career has taken off to another level; his performances have taken off to another planet, and his image and price tag have gone in the same direction.

Since his international debut in September 2020, Jack has lit up the English football team and now everyone is seeing why every Villa fan loves Jack Grealish. Being picked for the Euros transported Jack into the limelight even more, and his cameo roles have done his reputation no harm whatsoever, so much so that England fans are now disappointed at not seeing Jack in the starting line-up.

Moreover, when his name is announced or he is warming up, ready to come off the bench, there's always a chorus of, "Super, Super Jack..." ringing out from the England fans.

That is testament to how far Jack has progressed in his career and that will only improve with time.

Meanwhile, off the pitch, Jack initially gave the wrong impression of himself, with some unfortunate 'incidents' that could have sent his football career in the wrong direction, but fortunately, Jack learned his lessons and has conquered the wrong doings of his past. In fact, he banished his early 'bad boy' image in a split second, on the pitch at St Andrews on a sunny afternoon in March 2019, when a spectator ran on the pitch and attacked Jack. His reaction that day was exemplary in that he didn't react at all and carried on as if nothing had happened. Moreover, Jack won the day by scoring the only goal to win the game for Villa. It truly was a heroic performance by Jack in every way, shape or form.

Fast-forward to August 2021 and Jack has become the most expensive footballer in Britain. It was no fluke and it was well-deserved. He has matured as a footballer and, although the price-tag is huge, I'm sure that won't affect him or his game. Seeing Jack Grealish in a sky-blue shirt and not a claret and blue shirt is both painful and heart-warming at the same time. Painful in that he no longer plays for Villa, but heart-warming knowing Aston Villa have made him the most expensive footballer in Britain.

Jack is not just a fantastic footballer – he seems to be a genuine person who cares for others less fortunate than himself. For many years, Jack has been consistently helpful and charitable to certain people who are less fortunate or who's lives touch his heart. You see a side of Jack that isn't given much publicity, a side that tells me this guy is the real deal, on and off the pitch. I have captured some of the generosity of Jack Grealish, there's probably more that has gone unnoticed, not publicised or simply we just don't know about, so Jack Grealish is a superstar in my eyes, both as a footballer (regardless of who he plays for) and as a human being.

Simon Goodyear.

CLUB RECORD

Season	Division	Club	League *			Cups**			Total		
			Apps	Assts	Goals	Apps	Assts	Goals	Apps	Assts	Goals
2013/2014	League One	Notts County	37	5	5	0	0	0	37	5	5
2013/2014	Premier League	Aston Villa	1	0	0	0	0	0	1	0	0
2014/2015	Premier League	Aston Villa	17	1	0	7	3	0	24	4	0
2015/2016	Premier League	Aston Villa	16	0	1	5	2	0	21	2	1
2016/2017	Champion-ship	Aston Villa	31	2	5	2	0	0	33	2	5
2017/2018	Champion-ship	Aston Villa	30	7	3	1	0	0	31	7	3
2018/2019	Champion-ship	Aston Villa	31*	6	6	1	0	0	32	6	6
2019/2020	Premier League	Aston Villa	36	6	8	5	2	2	41	8	10
2020/2021	Premier League	Aston Villa	26	10	6	1	0	1	27	10	7
Totals			225	37	34	22	7	3	247	44	37

*Includes: Play-off semi-finals and final
** Includes: FA Cup, League Cup, 'Other' and

INTERNATIONAL RECORD

Country	Under-21			Full		
	Apps	Subs	Goals	Apps	Subs	Goals
Ireland	4	2	1	0	0	0
England	4	3	2	9	6	0
Totals	8	5	3	9	6	0

As of 10 September 2021

Also available:

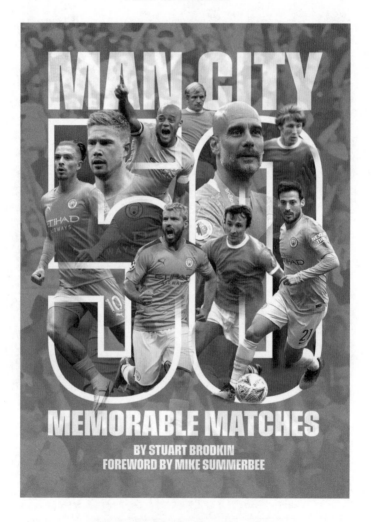

www.g2books.co.uk

Also available:

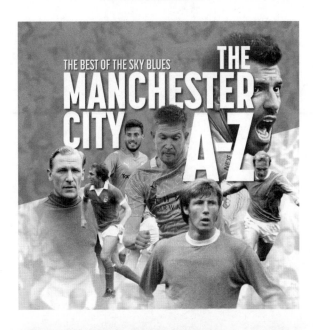

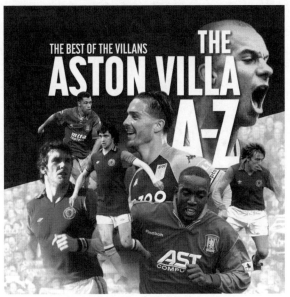